T

Know

 hrc

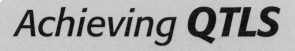

Achieving **QTLS**

The Minimum Core for
Language and
Literacy:
Knowledge, Understanding
and Personal Skills

Nancy Appleyard
Keith Appleyard

LearningMatters

First published in 2009 by Learning Matters Ltd

British Library Cataloguing in Publication Data
A CIP record for this book is available from the British Library.

ISBN 978 1 84445 212 5

Cover design by Topics – The Creative Partnership
Text design by Code 5
Project management by Deer Park Productions, Tavistock, Devon
Typeset by Pantek Arts Ltd, Maidstone, Kent
Printed and bound in Great Britain by Bell & Bain Ltd, Glasgow

Learning Matters Ltd
33 Southernhay East
Exeter EX1 1NX
Tel: 01392 215560
info@learningmatters.co.uk
www.learningmatters.co.uk

Mixed Sources
Product group from well-managed
forests and other controlled sources
www.fsc.org Cert no. TT-COC-002769
© 1996 Forest Stewardship Council

FSC

Contents

Acknowledgements

We would to thank the following for their help and support:

Lynn Senior, Peter Scales, Jenny Marshall and the ITT trainees at the University of Derby;

Eileen Gartside and the ITT trainees at New College, Stamford;

Ian and Helen Appleyard;

Rachel Brooks;

Mary Grange;

Paul Senior;

Mary Newman;

Susan Wallace;

Clare Weaver.

The author and publisher would like to thank the following for permission to reproduce copyright material:

Adapted and reproduced by permission of Hodder and Stoughton Ltd (page 73); Lynne Truss, *Eats, Shoots and Leaves*, 2003, Profile (page 118).

Every effort has been made to trace the copyright holders and to obtain their permission for the use of copyright material. The publisher and author will gladly receive any information enabling them to rectify any error or omission in subsequent editions.

1
Introduction

On 14 July 1865, Edward Whymper and six companions made the first successful ascent of the Matterhorn, an iconic mountain in the Swiss Alps which, until then, had been regarded as unclimbable. This was a feat of outstanding endurance, strength, co-operation and will-power, which confirmed Whymper's reputation as a leading mountaineer of his day. His success inspired thousands of mountain climbers, and nowadays the ascent of the Matterhorn is a difficult, but almost routine climb that is made by hundreds of climbers every year.

There are several reasons for this change from an epic to an everyday event. To begin with, the routes are now well known and there are expert guides. But perhaps the most important reason is the availability of tools and equipment that would be almost unrecognisable to Whymper. Boots, clothing, ropes, ice axes, tents have developed to an extent that makes the venture practicable for any serious mountaineer. If today's climbers were forced to use the tools and equipment that Whymper used, they might well succeed, but the task would be immeasurably more difficult.

So what has this to do with language and literacy in the context of lifelong learning? I think that there are some close parallels. Just as climbers would struggle to reach a summit using limited nineteenth-century tools, there are learners who struggle to gain qualifications because they have limited language and literacy tools; their ability to read, write, speak and listen is holding them back. And this is well documented. The Moser Report (DfEE, 1999) concluded that one in every five adults had literacy skills at a level below those expected of an 11-year-old, and the scale of the problem is reinforced by other research.

> *Over seven million adults in England have difficulties with literacy ... This means that they are unable to read and write very well and have difficulty doing some of the simplest tasks such as writing a letter (or) reading a piece of text – tasks that most of us take for granted.*
>
> (DfES, 2001, p5)

There are two other less obvious, but equally important, issues. Firstly, many learners who have overall good language and literacy skills can struggle with particular aspects: there is the graduate who is well capable of writing a thesis but is anxious and under-confident about giving a presentation; there is the A-level English student who has never quite grasped how to use apostrophes. So, it's probably not too much to say that most of the learners you meet will need some help to improve at least one or two aspects of their literacy skills. Secondly, we need to be sure as teachers that our own skills are as well developed as possible. To continue the mountaineering metaphor, we are the expert guides who know the routes, and our own tools need to be the very best possible.

One important task within teacher training in the learning and skills sector is to ensure that teachers have adequate language and literacy skills to do their job professionally. Another is to enable them to support their learners as they develop their reading, writing, speaking and listening skills. This is one reason why the minimum core of language and literacy has been introduced and the aim of this book is to help you to put it into practice.

Language, literacy and the minimum core

Let me begin by explaining what the minimum core of language and literacy actually is and how it will be covered in the main chapters of this book. The title of the book includes the words *minimum core* and *language and literacy* so it would seem reasonable to decide what these phrases actually mean. We can begin with a definition of the word *language.* According to the Oxford English Dictionary, *language* is defined as:

> *Words and the methods of combining them for the expression of thought. The act of speaking or talking, the use of speech.*

This definition tells us that language is how we use words, and the emphasis here is on the spoken word. This is useful for us because it shows that the minimum core places as much emphasis on speaking as on reading and writing.

Now, a definition of the word *literacy*:

> *Each individual is confident and capable when using the skills of speaking, listening, reading and writing and is able to communicate effectively, adapting to the range of audiences and contexts*
>
> (Definition of functional literacy, CBI, 2006, p104)

This definition is helpful too. To begin with, it states clearly what is involved, i.e., the skills of speaking, listening, reading and writing. However, unlike the definition of *language*, which describes doing something, i.e., using words, *literacy* is a measure of how well we are able to do this. The definition also describes the literate individual: someone who is confident and capable. You would expect to see here some measure of level of ability in these skills and the word *capable* fits the bill very well. But the definition also alludes to confidence. The literate individual is *confident* in their ability to perform these skills.

Just consider for a moment what this actually means. Imagine not having the confidence to fill in a form or feeling anxious whenever you have to write a letter. Imagine being a learner and being terrified because you have discovered that at some point you will be expected to speak in front of others. Many of these learners will have struggled with literacy at school; they may have a lifetime of coping with the stigma of poor language skills. For those of us with well-developed language and literacy skills, it isn't so easy to imagine what this must be like. But we do know that when someone is under-confident in language and literacy it can have a huge effect on their self-confidence and self-esteem.

Minimum core documents

The minimum core was first identified in 2004, and defined a minimum level of knowledge and competency in language, literacy and numeracy for all teachers in the lifelong learning sector. It was introduced into teacher education programmes in the same year, and was revised in 2007 as part of the reform agenda for teacher education, the majority of these revisions affecting numeracy and the introduction of ICT into the core.

The minimum core now has to be included in all Initial Teacher Training (ITT) programmes that have been developed as qualifications for teachers in the learning and skills sector. The relevant qualifications are the Certificate in Teaching in the Lifelong Learning Sector (CTLLS) for the associate teacher role, and the Diploma in Teaching in the Lifelong Learning Sector (DTLLS) for the full teaching role. These qualifications are often embedded in university PGCE and Certificate in Education courses. The minimum core requirement is included in the second Lifelong Learning UK (LLUK) unit of assessment (Planning and enabling learning) for the CTLLS, and in three units of assessment (Planning and enabling learning; Enabling learning and assessment; Theories and principles for planning and enabling learning) for the DTLLS.

The scope of the minimum core is detailed in the LLUK document *Addressing literacy, language, numeracy and ICT needs in education and training: defining the minimum core of teachers' knowledge, understanding and personal skills,* issued in June 2007. This document gives details of:

> *the knowledge, understanding and personal skills in English, Mathematics and ICT that teachers need to undertake their professional role, providing a developmental model on which teachers can build*
>
> (LLUK, November 2007, p2)

LLUK has also published a companion guide called *Inclusive Learning Approaches for Literacy, Language, Numeracy and ICT,* issued in November 2007. (For simplicity, I will refer to these two documents throughout as the minimum core document and the companion guide.) The companion guide supports the minimum core document and offers practical advice on implementing the minimum core aims and collaborative working with specialist teachers of literacy and language. It also provides signposts to some useful resource materials.

The language and literacy minimum core comprises 30 elements which are grouped in two parts. Part A covers knowledge and understanding of language and literacy and is sub-divided into two sections:

- factors affecting language and literacy learning;
- explicit knowledge of language and the four skills of speaking, listening, reading and writing.

Part B covers the personal language skills of speaking, listening, reading and writing. You can find details of the structure and elements at the end of this book in Appendix 1.

The introduction of the minimum core has resulted in a greater emphasis being placed on literacy within ITT programmes. Its aims have been twofold; firstly to develop trainees' language and literacy skills, and secondly to encourage the development of learners' language and literacy skills within a subject specialism. These two aims are important so we'll look at each in turn.

Developing your language and literacy skills

Firstly, as a teacher in the lifelong learning sector you will need a minimum level of knowledge and competency in language and literacy. So, what is this minimum level? In July 2008 LLUK issued a position statement, *Evidencing the personal skills requirements for teachers, tutors and trainers in the lifelong learning sector,* which sets out the minimum requirement at level 2 of the National Qualifications Framework (NQF)/Qualifications Credit Framework (QCF). Qualifications at level 2 include GCSE English A–C, The National Literacy Test, level 2, and Key Skills Communication, level 2. It emphasises that the level 2 skills are a minimum. It also stresses that many teachers will already have developed, or will need to develop, their skills above this in order to teach their specialist subject.

Developing the language and literacy skills of your learners

The second aim, teaching the minimum core within a subject specialism, is about how you, as a specialist teacher in your own subject area, can incorporate language and literacy naturally within your subject. You may feel that language and literacy are not relevant to your subject area, but they are, whatever your subject specialism. You are not expected to become a specialist language and literacy teacher, only to be able to identify, and take advantage of, opportunities within your subject for your learners to develop their language and literacy skills. To do this effectively you will need to be aware, not only of the literacy and language needs of your learners, but of the personal, cultural and social factors which have affected, and continue to affect, their language and literacy development. What does this actually mean?

Diversity and inclusive learning approaches

Perhaps more than anything, it means diversity. Each learner has a unique language and literacy profile. Each learner's economic, cultural and educational background will have influenced the way they have developed their language and literacy skills, their motivation and their attitude to learning. Some learners will have limited skills that may adversely affect their achievement in their learning subject. This is highlighted in the companion guide:

> *Teachers of all areas of specialism in the lifelong learning sector increasingly work with learners whose literacy (and) language ... skills are below level two of the Qualifications and Credit Framework (QCF). Learners' difficulties in these areas can be a barrier to achievement of their goals*
>
> (LLUK, November 2007, p2)

Other learners may not see the relevance of developing their language and literacy skills except within the context of work or when studying a specific subject. This is important. Just think for a moment about the opportunity this presents. Learners may not have succeeded with traditional literacy teaching but may well find literacy relevant and meaningful within the context of their subject area.

Let's return to the companion guide to look at what this means for us. The companion guide emphasises that we, as teachers, need to recognise the importance of English in enabling learners to achieve their subject goals. It gives the following examples of how and why learners need language skills:

- to access knowledge about an area of specialism;
- to acquire skills in a workplace context;
- to develop skills in an area of specialism;
- to prove achievement;
- to express individuality;
- for thinking, reasoning and understanding requirements and learning needs.

These examples represent a substantial proportion of learner activity time. Each one provides us with an opportunity to support learners in their language and literacy development.

Diversity also means that you are likely to have learners with very specific language and literacy skills, learners for whom English is not their first language and learners who may have specific difficulties, such as dyslexia or poor hearing, that can affect their language and literacy development. The needs of each of these learners will have to be met.

There is one more thing to consider. In addition to the diversity in skills within a group of learners, each learner may well have an uneven profile in terms of their competency across the range of language and literacy knowledge and skills, gaps in ability or confidence in one or more discrete areas. This uneven, or spiky profile, as it is often called, also needs to be identified and accommodated.

It is no coincidence that the title of the companion guide begins with the word *inclusive*. The need to ensure that all learners are given the best possible opportunity to fulfil their aspirations, that nobody should be excluded because of under-developed language and literacy skills, is a theme that runs constantly through all the minimum core documents and also through this book. In all the chapters I have focused on inclusive approaches that will address the language and literacy needs of your learners. Let's now have a look at how the book is organised.

About this book

In general terms, the book follows the sequence of the minimum core as detailed in the minimum core document. Thus, the first part of the book covers the knowledge and understanding elements of the core, while the second part deals with personal skills.

There are 12 chapters. You will find that the majority of the chapters follow a similar format. This format includes:

- links to the minimum core elements, to the relevant LLUK professional standards and to the relevant LLUK units of assessment;
- an introduction that briefly outlines the content of the chapter;
- strategies to develop your language and literacy skills and to support your learners as they develop their language and literacy skills;
- reflective and practical tasks;
- case studies and scenario studies;
- a summary of the key points covered;
- branching options at the end of each chapter, for consolidation and further research;
- references and further reading.

Chapter 2 is aimed at helping you to identify strengths and gaps in your understanding of language and literacy and your personal language and literacy skills. It will highlight areas for you to develop in order to meet the requirements of the minimum core. It includes a self-assessment questionnaire for you to complete, and suggested answers.

Chapters 3, 4, 5 and 6 cover background knowledge of the personal, social and cultural factors that influence language and literacy learning and development, including barriers to learning and multilingualism.

Chapters 7, 8, 9, 10 and 11 are concerned with the knowledge and practical skills of speaking, listening, non-verbal communication, reading, writing, grammar, punctuation and spelling.

The final chapter, Chapter 12, gives you guidance on ways you can develop your understanding of language and literacy in your future professional life.

In the Appendices at the end of the book you will find a summary of the minimum core, a grid to show how it is covered in this book and a glossary.

About the tasks

You will find both practical and reflective tasks throughout the book. Answers to most of the practical tasks are provided immediately after the task or in the text that follows. In the reflective tasks you are asked to consider certain points, to think about your own experience, or to imagine a situation. There are no so-called correct answers but you should certainly record your responses to them in your reflective journal.

At the end of most chapters you will find three tasks under the heading Branching Options, which are designed to help you consolidate and develop what you have learnt. These are classified as reflection, analysis and research tasks. The reflection option requires you to think about a particular aspect of the chapter and relate it to your own practice. The analysis option asks you to analyse specific incidents – usually from your own experience – and to relate these to the concepts discussed in the chapter. Finally, the research option gives you the opportunity to explore and develop these concepts in relation to your own professional practice.

About you

How you use this book depends, to a large extent, on who you are and what you want from it. As a reader, you will have some things in common with other readers. You are likely to be connected to the teaching profession in some way, probably in the lifelong learning sector, and you are also likely to be a specialist in your own field. You may be a newly qualified teacher, a trainee working towards QTLS, or a teacher trainer. If you are in a teaching role, your teaching subject could be anything from accountancy to zoology and it could be in a variety of settings. For example, you could be teaching in an adult education setting, an FE college, the National Health Service, in industry and so on. In addition, your preparation for your present role could have encompassed many years of practical experience. On the other hand it might have included study, which may, or may not, have been to an advanced level.

You will therefore want and need different things from your reading. If you are a trainee you will probably want to work your way through the book. You will want to take time to complete the assessment questionnaire in Chapter 2 to highlight any gaps in your knowledge and skills and use what you have discovered to direct your reading. If you are already in a teaching role you might want to dip in, focusing on the chapters that plug a gap either in your own skills and knowledge, or that of your learners. If you are a teacher trainer you might want to make use of some of the reflective and practical tasks to reinforce certain points or the branching options to consolidate your trainees' learning.

I have kept you very much in mind as I have been writing. My intention has been to make the tasks and scenarios appealing and relevant to you, but at the same time, to describe real experiences and to allow others to talk honestly about their experience.

REFERENCES AND FURTHER READING REFERENCES AND FURTHER READING

CBI (2006) *Working on the three Rs; priorities for functional skills in maths and English*. London: CBI.

DfEE (1999) *A Fresh Start – Improving Literacy and Numeracy* (the Moser Report). London: DfEE.

DfES (2001) *Adult Literacy Core Curriculum*. London: DfES.

Evans, N (2003) *Making sense of lifelong learning*. London: Routledge.

LLUK (June 2007) *Addressing literacy, language, numeracy and ICT needs in education and training: defining the minimum core of teachers' knowledge, understanding and personal skills.* London: LLUK (the minimum core document).

LLUK (November 2007) *Inclusive learning approaches for literacy, language, numeracy and ICT.* London: LLUK (the companion guide).

LLUK (2008) *Evidencing the personal skills requirements for teachers, tutors and trainers in the lifelong learning sector.* London: LLUK.

2
Self-assessment

This chapter will help you to:

• **assess your knowledge and level of skill in language and literacy.**

Links to minimum core elements:
All elements. (See Appendix A for details.)

Links to LLUK Professional Standards for QTLS:
AS4, AS7, AK4.2, AK4.3, AP4.2, BS2, BK2.3, BP2.2, BP2.3, BK3.1, BK3.2, BK3.3, BP3.1, BP3.2, BP3.3, CK3.3, CK3.4, CP3.3, CP3.4.

Links to LLUK mandatory units of assessment:
Planning and enabling learning (CTLLS and DTLLS):
• **understand and demonstrate knowledge of the minimum core in own practice.**

Enabling learning and assessment (DTLLS):
• **understand and demonstrate knowledge of the minimum core in own practice;**
• **understand how to evaluate and improve own assessment practice.**

Introduction

One of the first things for you to think about is assessing your language and literacy knowledge and skills with regard to the requirements of the minimum core. It is also important for you to assess how confident you feel about your language and literacy skills, so that you can support your learners more effectively. Before you make a start, it is worth looking again at the minimum core requirements. We can summarise them in the following statements.

You need to have:

• an understanding of the personal, social and cultural factors influencing language and literacy learning and development;
• explicit knowledge about language and the four skills: speaking, listening, reading and writing;
• a minimum level of competency in your personal language skills of speaking, listening, reading and writing.

This chapter comprises a self-assessment questionnaire and suggested answers concerning the aspects of language and literacy detailed in the minimum core. Don't expect to answer all the questions correctly or even, necessarily, to achieve a high score. Be kind to yourself, use the questionnaire to give you a flavour of what the minimum core is about, to identify your overall strengths and highlight the areas you want to develop.

The questionnaire is in two parts. These mirror the minimum core, as detailed in the minimum core document. Part A is concerned with your knowledge and understanding of the personal, social and cultural issues associated with language and literacy, and your knowledge about language and the four skills of speaking, listening, reading and writing. Part B covers your personal language skills for teaching and professional life.

You may have already undertaken a diagnostic assessment at the start of your programme. If so, you can use what you discover from this questionnaire to complement what you already know. Once you have identified the areas you wish to develop, you should note these, probably in your learning journal, and incorporate them in your individual learning plan (ILP).

Self-assessment questionnaire
Part A: knowledge and understanding

Part A is divided into:

- A1 – Personal, social and cultural issues associated with language and literacy;
- A2 – Explicit knowledge about language and of the four skills: speaking, listening, reading and writing.

A1 – Personal, social and cultural issues associated with language and literacy

This covers:

- factors that affect the acquisition and development of language and literacy skills;
- the importance of English language and literacy in enabling users to participate in public life, society and the modern economy;
- potential barriers and learning difficulties;
- multilingualism and varieties of English.

Write down your answers to the following 15 questions and compare them to the suggested responses given after the questions. Bear in mind that there are no absolutely right or wrong answers. Rather, the intention is to provoke thought on the issues and enable you to reflect on how they relate to your teaching experience. Note in your journal those areas where you are not confident of the depth of your knowledge or understanding. All these topics are covered in detail in Chapters 3–6 of this book.

1 In what ways do you think the way you speak is a part of your identity?
2 Do you think that women use language differently from men? If so, in what way?
3 What reasons can you think of for someone having limited literacy skills?
4 What additional barriers might older people face in developing their literacy skills?
5 Do you believe that improving technology has lessened or increased the need for good basic skills?
6 What do you understand by the term social exclusion?
7 Can you think of any ways that limited language and literacy skills might affect mental wellbeing?
8 How does the Special Educational Needs and Disability Act (2001) affect education providers and learners in the lifelong learning sector?

9   In what ways might poor hearing affect a learner in the classroom?
10 How could you give support to learners who are very anxious about their language and literacy skills?
11 What is Standard English? Are there other varieties of spoken English that are also correct?
12 How does accent differ from dialect?
13 In what ways could ESOL learners be at a disadvantage?
14 What is the citizenship test?
15 In what circumstances might it be appropriate to use slang?

Suggested answers for Part A1 – Personal, social and cultural issues associated with language and literacy

These answers indicate a range of possible responses, but are not comprehensive. If you have given other answers, you may well be right, so check with the relevant chapter.

1   Some examples of how your speech reflects your identity are:
    • your accent;
    • sound of your voice;
    • your vocabulary;
    • your language style.
2   Yes, women and men do use language differently. Some examples are:
    • women tend to use polite phrases more often than men, for example, *may I have*?
    • women are more likely to initiate conversation;
    • men tend to interrupt more often.
3   There are many different reasons for limited literacy skills. Some examples include:
    • low level of motivation;
    • unhappy experiences at school;
    • low expectations.
4   Some additional barriers for older people include:
    • health problems, for example poor sight/hearing;
    • labelling of older people as slower to learn;
    • anxiety about using information technology;
    • unfamiliar teaching/learning strategies.
5   The need for good basic skills has not lessened as technology has improved. According to the adult literacy core curriculum, good basic skills are even more essential.
6   Social exclusion is a term used to describe a lack of access to information and/or support that could assist people into better housing, jobs, education, etc.
7   Limited language and literacy skills can lower confidence and self-esteem.
8   The Special Educational Needs and Disability Act (2001) states that no learner should be treated less favourably because of a particular difficulty. Educational organisations must make reasonable adjustments to ensure that disabled people in education do not suffer a substantial disadvantage in comparison to people who are not disabled. For most types of education provider, making *reasonable adjustments* can include changes to practices or procedures, changes to physical features and providing extra support (such as specialist teachers or equipment).
9   Poor hearing could affect a learner in a number of ways, for example:
    • they might not understand instructions or explanations immediately;
    • they might be anxious participating in discussions;
    • they might find it difficult to build relationships with other members of the class.
10 Learners who are very anxious about language and literacy would need ongoing reassurance, and tasks that provide opportunities for them to be successful.
11 There are a number of varieties of English of which Standard English is only one: these varieties are different but not necessarily inferior.

12 Dialect refers to differences in vocabulary and grammar associated with a particular region. Accent refers to the way words are pronounced.

13 ESOL (English for Speakers of Other Languages) learners can be at a disadvantage because of cultural differences and unfamiliar teaching environments. However, ESOL learners may well have grammar and language skills in their first language, which can assist them in expressing themselves in another language.

14 The citizenship test is a social history and cultural test for foreigners who wish to become British citizens.

15 Slang can sometimes be very useful for conveying meaning and is acceptable in informal situations. It is normally inappropriate in a teaching situation because some learners might not understand its meaning and could feel excluded.

A2 – Explicit knowledge about language and of the four skills: speaking, listening, reading and writing

Write down your answers to the following 15 questions and check them against the answers that are given after the questions. Note those areas where you are not confident of the depth of your knowledge. All these topics are covered in detail in Chapters 7–11 of this book.

1 What is a closed question?
2 What do you understand by the term *paraphrase*?
3 What is colloquial language?
4 Within the context of interpersonal communication, what do you understand by the terms *proximity* and *orientation*?
5 What is the Dewey system?
6 What do you understand by the term *critical reading*?
7 Give an example of a textual feature.
8 What is the Harvard system?
9 What is the difference between a bibliography, an index, a glossary and an appendix?
10 What headings might you use for the different sections of a report for a project or an assignment?
11 In a sentence, what is the job of a conjunction?
12 What is the meaning of the following words?
   • *syntax*
   • *homophone*
   • *simile*
13 Do you agree with both, one, or neither of the following statements?
   • *A sentence contains a subject and a verb*.
   • *A sentence expresses a complete thought*.
14 The following sentence contains at least one noun, pronoun, verb, adverb, adjective, and preposition. Can you identify them?
   • *They saw many tiny crabs scuttling rapidly across the sand*.
15 What is the difference between descriptive and reflective writing?

Answers for Part A2 – Explicit knowledge about language and of the four skills: speaking, listening, reading and writing

1 A closed question allows the recipient the option of only a short, often yes/no, answer. Examples of closed questions are: *Do you understand? What is the capital of...?*
2 *Paraphrase*: to express the meaning of something using different words.
3 Colloquial language is an informal style of speaking.
4 *Proximity* is the distance between others and ourselves; *orientation* is our position in relation to others.

5   The Dewey system is a reference system for classifying books.
6   *Critical reading* means not just accepting the content of a piece of writing but questioning its logic and validity.
7   Punctuation, grammar, style and format are examples of textual features.
8   The Harvard system is the most frequently used referencing system for written material.
9   A bibliography is a list of reference material used in research, placed either at the end of each chapter or at the end of the book.
     An index is an alphabetical list of topics, usually at the end of a book.
     A glossary is a collection of technical or specialised words.
     An appendix is a subsidiary addition, usually to a book.
10 A report for a project or assignment could include some, or all, of the following headings: title, abstract, table of contents, introduction/rationale, methods, main body, conclusions, recommendations, appendices, references/bibliography.
11 A conjunction is a word that joins parts of a sentence, for example, *and*, *but*.
12 *Syntax*: the grammatical arrangement of words in a sentence.
     Homophone: a word that sounds the same as another but which has a different spelling and a different meaning, for example, *through/threw or plaice/place*.
     Simile: a comparison introduced by the words *like* or *as*, for example, *as tall as a steeple*.
13 Both statements are correct.
14 Nouns   *crabs, sand*
     Pronoun   *they*
     Verbs   *saw, scuttling*
     Adverb   *rapidly*
     Adjectives   *many, tiny, the*
     Preposition   *across*
15 Descriptive writing describes an event (or concept), for example, *Yesterday I explained the assignment to the learners*. Reflective writing reflects back on what happened and raises questions, for example, *How clearly did I explain the assignment?* or *Could everyone hear me?*

Self-assessment questionnaire
Part B: Personal language skills

This part of the questionnaire covers your personal language skills for teaching and professional life for:

- speaking and listening;
- non-verbal communication;
- reading;
- writing;
- grammar, punctuation and spelling.

There are two batches of questions in this part of the questionnaire. The first batch of 15 questions should enable you to assess your confidence in your personal language skills. The second batch comprises a personal skills audit.

Batch A – Assessment of confidence

The following 15 questions are aimed at helping you to make your own judgement about how you feel about your language and literacy skills. The questions ask you to assess how confident or capable you feel in a number of different situations. It is a good idea to answer them using the following scoring system:

completely confident/capable:	score 4;
reasonably confident/capable:	score 3;
not too confident/capable:	score 2;
not at all confident/capable:	score 1.

How confident do you feel that you:

- can give an effective presentation to a large group of people?
- can adapt your speaking appropriately to support ESOL learners and learners with a range of disabilities?
- can speak clearly and fluently to all the audiences in your teaching role?
- have an awareness of your non-verbal signals?
- are generally sensitive to the non-verbal signals of others?
- indicate to learners that you listen to them carefully?
- use strategies in your teaching to encourage your learners to listen effectively?
- understand and practise active listening?
- are a fluent and active reader?
- are a capable researcher (including internet research) with a consistent strategy for making effective notes from your research material?
- are thorough in proof reading your work and identifying errors?
- are a confident and fluent writer, able to use appropriate language for a variety of different audiences?
- are able to write clearly, using well-constructed paragraphs and sentences?
- are able to punctuate your sentences correctly?
- are able to spell correctly?

When you analyse your score, you should be able to identify a preliminary profile of your personal language and literacy skills. You can use this in conjunction with your answers to the following skills audit.

Batch B – Skills audit

Write down the answers to the following 10 questions, and compare them to the suggested responses given after the questions. This should give you an indication of any areas where you need to focus and develop your own language and literacy skills.

1 How would you avoid plagiarism when making notes?
2 How would you indicate verbally that you are listening attentively when someone is speaking to you?
3 What non-verbal signals would you give to show that you are listening when someone is speaking to you?
4 How would you interpret the following non-verbal signals?
  - A learner is sitting talking with arms crossed in front, as in a self-hug, following your explanation of a task.
  - A colleague makes infrequent eye contact when you ask for advice.
  - Some learners are sitting in a small group around a table, leaning towards each other.
5. Are any of the following sentences passive?
  - *Bob was hungry*.
  - *The dog was walked*.
  - *Your signature is required*.
6. Which of the following statements are sentences?
  - *As soon as we arrived, we went to bed*.
  - *As we have been accustomed to in the past*.
  - *An idyllic house, located near the sea, surrounded by a beautiful garden*.
  - *John left early*.

7. What is wrong with the following sentences?
   - *A group of learners are working hard.*
   - *There were less people attending the evening performance.*
   - *These books are a present from Jo and I.*
8. How would you punctuate the following sentences?
   - *This english book has lost its cover*
   - *Todays session covered spelling punctuation and grammar*
   - *Hell come as soon as johns class has finished*
   - *Youre sure she wont mind if I use her pens he asked*
9. Which is the correct spelling?
   - *baught*   *bought*   *bawt*
   - *benafit*   *benefit*   *benifit*
   - *maintenence*   *maintenense*   *maintenance*
   - *competent*   *compatent*   *competant*
   - *ecercise*   *exercise*   *exersise*
   - *wether*   *wheather*   *whether*
   - *relevant*   *relevent*   *relavent*
   - *professional*   *proffessional*   *prefesional*
   - *sinserely*   *sincerely*   *sincerly*
10. Which word is correct in order for each of the following sentences to make sense?
    - *She had to* accept/except *that she couldn't do everything.*
    - *One possible* affect/effect *of global warming is a rise in sea levels.*
    - *We watched a* current/currant *affairs programme.*
    - *The barrister was able to* elicit/illicit *the full facts from the witness.*
    - Formally/formerly, *we had to wait outside; now we can go straight in.*

Answers to Batch B - Skills audit (C)

1. Use your own words to make notes and carefully note the reference material details.
2. Use verbal cues such as I *see*, and Go *on*.
3. Frequent eye contact, nods and smiles.
4. The learner might be feeling anxious.
    Your colleague might be in a hurry or not wish to talk.
    The members of the group will be fully engaged in their activity.
5. The second and third sentences are passive.
6. The first and fourth statements are sentences.
7. *A group of learners* is *working hard.*
    There were fewer *people attending the evening performance.*
    These books are a present from Jo and me.
8. *This English book has lost its cover.*
    Today's session covered spelling, punctuation and grammar.
    He'll come as soon as John's class has finished.
    'You're sure she won't mind if I use her pens?' he asked.
9. *bought, benefit, maintenance, competent, exercise, whether, relevant,*
    professional, sincerely.
10. *accept, effect, current, elicit, formerly.*

Where next?

You should now be able to identify and note those areas of personal knowledge and skills of speaking, listening, reading and writing that you feel you need to develop. This will be the focus of your attention as you work through the chapters of the book. You might find an action plan helpful for closing specific gaps in your skills and knowledge, possibly included within your overall course action plan. The important thing is to make sure that your plan is effective. Using a SMART action plan may help you to do this.

The SMART action plan

SMART is an acronym used as a model to help people set and reach their goals. It stands for:

Specific, Measurable, Attainable, Relevant, Time-bound.

Specific
Have you clearly defined your goal? Be as precise as you can. For example, *Improve my spelling* is too vague. A better option would be, *Learn to spell ten difficult words*.

Measurable
Be clear as to how you will know that you have achieved your goal. For example, *Make a list of 10 difficult words and write them down correctly from memory.*

Attainable
Your goals need to be challenging but realistic, for example, *Set aside an hour on Saturday to learn 20 difficult words*, rather than, *Spend Saturday working on spelling*.

Relevant
Try to take a whole-view approach to setting goals. Ask yourself how relevant each one is to the overall picture. For instance, learn to spell technical words that will be used in your assignment, rather than selecting words at random.

Time-bound
Set yourself a date for achieving each goal. For example, *Make sure I am confident I can spell the 10 difficult words by Saturday.* This will help to keep you focused and motivated as you achieve each one.

As you move forward through your programme it is a good idea to monitor your progress. If you have made an action plan, remember to review it regularly, ticking off goals as you achieve them and writing in some new ones.

REFERENCES AND FURTHER READING REFERENCES AND FURTHER READING

LLUK (June 2007) *Addressing literacy, language, numeracy and ICT needs in education and training: defining the minimum core of teachers' knowledge, understanding and personal skills.* London: LLUK (the minimum core document).

3
Influences and attitudes

This chapter will help you to:

- **identify the factors that influence language learning;**
- **use theories of learning to understand learners' attitudes to language and literacy.**

Links to minimum core elements:

A 1.1   The different factors affecting the acquisition and development of language and literacy skills.

A 1.3   Potential barriers that can hinder development of language skills.

A 1.8   The importance of context in language use and the influence of the communicative situation.

Links to LLUK Professional Standards for QTLS:
AS3, AS4, AS7, AK3.1, AP3.1, AK4.1, AP4.1, BK2.2, BP2.2, BK2.3, BP2.3, BK3.1, BK3.2, BK3.3, BK3.4, BP3.1, BP3.2, BP3.3, BP3.4, CK3.4, CP3.4.

Links to LLUK mandatory units of assessment:
Planning and enabling learning (CTLLS and DTLLS):
- **understand how to plan for inclusive learning;**
- **understand how to use teaching and learning strategies and resources inclusively to meet curriculum requirements;**
- **understand and demonstrate knowledge of the minimum core in own practice.**

Theories and principles for planning and enabling learning (DTLLS):
- **understand the application of theories and principles of learning and communication to inclusive practice;**
- **understand how to apply theories and principles of learning and communication in planning and enabling inclusive learning;**
- **understand and demonstrate knowledge of the minimum core in own practice.**

Introduction

If I were to ask you to identify aspects or features of yourself that you feel form part of your identity and that enable other people to recognise you, you might immediately think of your facial features or the colour of your hair. It might take you a moment or two to realise that the way you speak, the sound of your voice, your vocabulary and your language style are also an essential part of your identity. Your family, school, neighbourhood and friendship groups will all have played a part in forming your identity, including the way you have developed your language.

When learners arrive in our classrooms they bring with them their own personal, unique experience of both language and literacy; this experience will have helped to form their attitudes to language and literacy learning. If we are to integrate language and literacy effectively into our teaching programmes, to enthuse all of our learners, we need to have an understanding of some of the factors involved in forming their attitudes.

In the first half of this chapter we will identify some of the personal, social and cultural factors that affect the acquisition and development of language and literacy. We will look specifically at the following aspects:

- theories of language acquisition;
- how development of language and literacy is influenced by:
  - socio-economic background;
  - gender;
  - peer group;
  - ethnicity;
  - motivation.

In the second part of this chapter we will use theories of learning to explore some of the attitudes that learners may have to language and literacy.

Theories of language acquisition

There are two major theories for how children acquire language: behaviourist theory and language acquisition device (LAD). These two theories are explored in detail in Child (1993), but here is a summary. Behaviourist theory suggests that children learn language through imitation and positive reinforcement. One example is the babbling sounds that babies make, being rewarded by the positive response of parents. LAD theory, put forward by Noam Chomsky, suggests that children have a language blueprint, an innate capacity for language learning. As evidence for this theory he asserts that all languages, from the simplest to the most complex, share a common structure.

> *Language learning is not really something that the child does; it is something that happens to the child placed in an appropriate environment, much as the child's body grows and matures in a predetermined way when provided with appropriate nutrition and environmental stimulation.*
>
> (Chomsky, cited in Fromkin et al 2003, p347)

Child proposes that it is likely that both these processes are involved in language acquisition. He goes on to say that although there is no generally accepted account of the relationship between language acquisition and cognition, or thought processes, it would be inconceivable to imagine that there is no connection. One example of this connection from Jean Piaget's work describes how children do not use comparative words such as *longer* and *shorter* before they are able to understand their meaning, that is, before they are able to line up a bunch of sticks in length order (Lowe and Graham, 1998).

Influences on language development

Language and literacy development is influenced by factors such as socio-economic background, gender, peer group, ethnicity and motivation. Let's look at these in turn.

Socio-economic background

An important study, relevant to us, looked into how a child's background affects language development. Basil Bernstein (1975) studied the systematic differences in the way children develop language by contrasting children from poorer and wealthier backgrounds. He found that children from a poorer socio-economic background used a restricted language code. Within the family circle, certain values and norms were taken for granted rather than being explained. Parents, for example, might discipline a child by using commands such as *No!* or *That's enough!* rather than explaining why behaviour is not acceptable. He suggested that a restricted code is more suitable for talking about practical matters rather than abstract ideas. By contrast, Bernstein found that children from a wealthier socio-economic background used an elaborated language code that enabled them to generalise and therefore express abstract ideas.

Gender

> *The growing body of studies on the language use of women in a variety of settings and cultural groups provides convincing evidence that differences will exist in the speech of men and women in every social group.*
>
> (Nichols, 1987, p108)

O'Barr and Atkins (1987) have identified a number of differences between men and women's language use. Women use more empty adjectives such as *lovely* or *sweet* while men are more likely to use swear words. Women use more tag questions, for example, *she's clever, isn't she?* and *that was interesting, wasn't it?* Women also tend to be more polite in their use of language.

Gender differences are not confined to spoken language. Women and men have marked preferences in their choice of reading material. Men are more attracted to factual material and to graphs and tables, whereas women are more attracted to fiction and find text more appealing than graphical representations. We can trace this difference in attitude to reading material back to childhood and the way boys and girls approach reading. On average, girls read more fluently than boys, learn to read earlier and are able to read faster (Shaw, 1995). Girls also seem to enjoy reading more than boys and choose to read stories while boys prefer comics and facts. Indeed, the marked preference of girls for English learning is reflected in the GCSE exam results where girls consistently attain higher grades. The Department of Children, Schools and Families (DCSF) education and training statistics for the UK 2007 show the following:

- GCSE English grades A–C: girls 71%; boys 56%;
- GCSE Literature grades A–C: girls 74%; boys 61%;
- GCSE Communication grades A–C: girls 65%; boys 50%.

Although developmental variations between girls and boys provide an explanation of these differences, social and cultural factors cannot be ignored. An unpublished small-scale study in two Lincolnshire schools questioned 59 children about their own feelings regarding reading (Brooks, Bishop Grosseteste College, 1993). The study revealed that almost all of the children questioned saw reading as a girl's activity but didn't see it as a boy's activity. This is hardly surprising as the study also showed that the majority of the children could recall many occasions of being read to by a female, (mothers, grandmothers, older sisters and female teachers) but only a few were able to recall occasions where they had been read to by a male.

PRACTICAL TASK PRACTICAL TASK PRACTICAL TASK PRACTICAL TASK PRACTICAL TASK

Observe a group of colleagues or friends in discussion. What differences do you notice between the speech of the men and the women? Note your observations and compare them to the findings of O'Barr and Atkins.

Peer group

... personal network structure is of great importance in any attempt to describe patterns of language use ... a dense, multiplex personal network structure predicts relative closeness to vernacular norms.

(Milroy, 1987, p81)

When Milroy talks about *personal network structure* he is referring to peer groups, for example work groups, age groups and interest groups. He goes on to say that each group will have its own language rules and vocabulary determined by the norms of the group. Lowe and Graham (1998) suggest that we gradually accommodate our language to the people around us to signal affinity with the group. We are also able to move effortlessly between groups. A group of young people, for example, might use swear words and slang openly to indicate group cohesion but, individually, have little difficulty using more formal or polite language at work or home. Because the language we use within these different groups confirms our sense of belonging, language can become a means of excluding others even if the exclusion is unconscious. For example, we can feel excluded if we use a dialect or speak with an accent that is different from the rest of the group.

Ethnicity

Ethnic background has a massive influence on attitudes to language and literacy.

CASE STUDY – HAI LING

Hai Ling is from Shanghai and she talks here about the cultural attitudes and expectations that exist in China.

Education in China is very different from education in England and so is our attitude to it. In China it is highly valued, especially being able to speak and write English. The grammar is drummed into us – I think I probably have a better understanding of English grammar than many English people. Our parents have to pay for our education and we all know that this is our one and only chance. There is the added pressure to do well so that we can support our parents when they are old as pensions are small and many people do not qualify.

We can see from Hai Ling's comments that some cultures place a high value on education and, specifically, on English.

REFLECTIVE TASK

Which group or groups would you say have most influenced the way you have developed your language: your family, your school, your neighbourhood, your ethnic group or your friends?

Has your language changed over time? If it has, what do you think has been responsible for this change?

Motivation

Our motivation for learning can influence our language and literacy development. This is illustrated in the following comments from two learners, the first from Linda.

CASE STUDY – LINDA

I was 53 years old when I returned to education. For as long as I could remember I had wanted to be a nurse but my parents had been against the idea; instead, I became a lab technician. After having a family I took part-time and casual work to fit in with school times but once my children had left home I began to think again about nursing.

Despite loving every minute of my course, my early weeks and months were full of anxiety about my ability to cope with what I was being asked to do. I didn't have any concerns about the practical aspects of the programme; I was confident that I could care for sick people. Not so with the academic element. I was constantly worried about my ability to understand some of the more technical nursing terms. My major worry, and one which dominated my thoughts and kept me awake at night, was whether I could manage to do the written assignments that the programme demanded. Was I bright enough to write assignments? After all, I'd written very little since school. More to the point, was I too old anyway to be doing anything academic?

I expect you can understand Linda's fears. After all, she was embarking on a major life change. From being a part-time casual worker, which probably required little more dedication than turning up when required and doing her job, she was taking on a substantial and demanding training programme with a view to a completely new career. But notice, it isn't the massive changes to her life that are giving her sleepless nights; it's her fear that she might be too old to write academic essays.

This is a very real fear for many older people, that as you get older you are less able to learn. And the fear is often born out of the negative prejudice that can be attached to economically inactive groups. Research into ageism has debunked this prejudice but does suggest that negative labelling itself can affect how well we perform (Rogers, 2007). If others have little confidence in our abilities we come to believe that they are right.

Linda has wrongly supposed that her age will affect her literacy skills and this belief has affected her self-confidence. But there is another important factor here: that of her motivation. She is strongly motivated to complete this course and start a new career. The clues to Linda's motivation are in the words, *always wanted to be a nurse*, and *loved every minute of the course*. Linda clearly wants to be learning and to succeed in her future career and her motivation is personal.

PRACTICAL TASK PRACTICAL TASK PRACTICAL TASK PRACTICAL TASK PRACTICAL TASK

Not all motivation is personal like Linda's. Make a list of any other factors that you think might provide motivation to succeed on a learning programme. Then compare your list with those you identify in the following comments from Peter.

CASE STUDY – PETER

I remember two books in my childhood home. They were both about woodwork and had some photographs of wood beams and joists. One of the photographs looked just like my infant school hall: when I was very small I thought someone had actually come into the school with a camera. I remember these two books well because they were the only books in the house.

I left school as soon as I could. I wasn't interested in all that writing stuff. I could read and write well enough, no problem there, but it was all a bit of a waste of time as I'd already got a job lined up. My teachers weren't all that interested in me anyway. I didn't blame them; they could tell I'd rather be anywhere but at school (I often was when I got the chance). Anyway my mum and dad wanted me to get a proper job and make a contribution to the household budget. And I was looking forward to starting work, along with my two best mates, at a local motor plant and earning some money.

I'd done well at work over the years; a couple of good promotions and I was now in a supervisory position. Then the company had been taken over and everything seemed to change. Now it was introducing a new management scheme so here I was, having to complete this course on Communication within the Organisation. I didn't really know why I was on the course, why they needed to introduce it in the first place and I certainly didn't see the point of it. Well, actually, the point for me was I had to complete the course because my line manager said so. After all, I didn't want to jeopardise my job; it would also mean a bit more money and Jane, my wife, was keen for me to get on. Even so, I knew that I would be spending a lot of time clock-watching.

Unlike Linda, Peter didn't want to be on the course. He didn't see things like reading and writing reports and making presentations as being relevant to his life. He'd never needed them and was unhappy with what was now expected of him by his employers. It was, for him, a monumental change and he was feeling pretty uncomfortable. His motivations, keeping his job, the extra money and keeping his wife happy, were instrumental rather than personal.

REFLECTIVE TASK

As you read Peter's story did you notice that his own expectations in terms of development of his language and literacy skills were very limited. Neither Peter nor his wider social network, his teachers, parents and peers, saw language and literacy skills as relevant to Peter. Why do you think this was?

For you, which do you believe is more powerful, personal or instrumental motivation? Why?

Theories of learning and attitudes to language and literacy

You are probably already very familiar with learning theories in the context of how you can apply them in the classroom. In this section we will see how they can help explain attitudes adult learners may have about language and literacy. You are likely to meet many learners who are enthusiastic and positive: equally, and sadly, you will meet learners who are resistant or even hostile. Some may not even recognise their resistance, let alone understand where it originates.

Behaviourist theory

As we saw earlier, at its simplest, behaviourist theory suggests that human behaviour is modified by reward (Child, 1993). The reward can be positive or negative. For example, if we get pleasure from reading we will want to read more. On the other hand, if we find reading a chore, given a choice, we'll find other activities more to our liking. Read what Jacob has to say about his experience of negative reward.

CASE STUDY – JACOB

I was about 11 or 12 at the time. The English teacher had been nagging us for weeks to be more creative in writing our weekly homework essay. I couldn't really work out what she meant by creative but I was determined to get a good mark for this particular essay entitled A Day in My Life*, so I let my mind wander to see if I could create something. What appeared was a story of meeting an alien who was just like me; he hated disgusting school dinners and was always fighting with his older brother. I can still remember the excruciating embarrassment when the English teacher threw my work on to my desk and told the whole class that it was* ridiculous and utter rubbish. *It took me years to feel comfortable about writing essays.*

REFLECTIVE TASK

Think about your own experiences of language and literacy. Can you identify any examples of positive or negative reward? What effect did this have on your attitude to language and literacy?

Cognitive theory

As we saw earlier, cognitive theorists such as Piaget stress the thinking element of human behaviour, suggesting a process more complex than simply responding to positive or negative reward (Lowe and Graham, 1998). Learners respond intelligently in a variety of contexts and are actively involved in selecting and adapting knowledge and in rejecting that which they see as not relevant. Mark's story illustrates this point.

CASE STUDY – MARK

I did well at school, achieving four A grades at GCE A level. It was sort of taken for granted that I would go on to university to study mechanical engineering and I must admit I liked the idea of getting a degree. It didn't take me long to realise that university had little meaning for me. I just wanted to be in the real world doing real work. I did manage to hang on for three years and scrape though my degree. I never did see any relevance to the discussions we had at university or the writing and reading we did, whereas now that I'm working I really enjoy the discussions I have with customers, writing up jobs and reading progress reports.

For Mark, language and literacy were only relevant in the context of a work environment; separated from this context they were meaningless. Even the reward of a degree was not enough to motivate him. This is important for us: learners do sometimes see literacy as meaningless. Developing literacy skills within subject learning will help to avoid this situation.

Humanist theory

Humanists focus on the relationship between the teacher and the learner. The teacher should be non-judgemental and try to make learners feel accepted and valued. Carl Rogers (1983) called this unconditional positive regard. This seems to us now to be a reasonable expectation, even if, for some learners, it takes a great deal of effort on our part.

Let us ponder for a moment on a different scenario, one where the concept of *unconditional positive regard* would have been incomprehensible. As teachers, we usually have little idea of the experiences many of our learners, particularly older learners, will have had during their school years. There will be people sitting in our classrooms who were educated during the 1950s. Discipline at that time was much more rigid than today. It would seem inconceivable to us now to read or hear of a teacher caning, or even smacking a child, yet for many older learners it was a fact of life, as you can see from Eve's experience.

CASE STUDY – EVE

Mrs Selton was very strict. We were never allowed to talk in class and I was always getting into trouble for breaking this rule. I can still remember her striding down the aisle towards my desk with her ruler in her hand. In the early weeks in her class I don't think I ever managed to go more than two or three days without feeling that ruler across the palm of my hand, but she cured me in the end.

Even in the more relaxed latter part of the twentieth century, acceptance of a learner's individual limitations could be far from unconditional. Here is Nelson's story.

CASE STUDY – NELSON

I wasn't in special needs or anything like that; in fact I ended up getting nine GCSEs and have even got an AS since. But there was one thing I really struggled with and it caused me no end of problems. The thing is I write very slowly. I'm a pretty untidy writer anyway and if I try and speed up no one can read it, not even me sometimes. The teachers never got it. They'd just keep going on at me to write more quickly and if I didn't finish my work I had to stay in and do it in break time. If I really tried to write as quickly as I could they'd moan at me because it was so scrawled. Doesn't make sense does it? I hate writing now, not because I write slowly but because they made me feel so bad about it.

REFLECTIVE TASK

How do you think that Eve and Nelson's school experiences will have affected their adult attitude to language and literacy?

These experiences show us that learners' confidence in their language and literacy skills can be severely undermined by negative experiences at school. Positive experiences, on the other hand, can have the opposite effect. Here are two more school memories, from Marian and Laura.

> ## CASE STUDY – MARIAN AND LAURA
>
> *Our teacher had the most beautiful handwriting. I loved to watch her write on the board; all the letters had curly bits, like old-fashioned writing. She taught us to write like that. Do you know, even now, when I write letters or send birthday cards, I write the way she taught us – I really enjoy it.*
>
> *Our teacher used to get us to take turns around the class reading from a story-book. One day she brought in a book called Moonfleet by John Falkner. It was the most amazing story, about Bluebeard and pirates and smuggling and that was it; I was hooked on reading – I just couldn't get enough.*

Marian and Laura's positive experiences of English at school have ensured their enjoyment of reading and writing as adults.

Learning through experience

We know that adults approach their learning with well-established beliefs and attitudes and a variety of life experiences. They have an awareness of their own responsibility in the process of learning; they are also more discriminating than children about which types of learning they like or don't like (Rogers, 2007). If given the opportunity, adults will choose learning experiences they see as providing what they need in an environment where they feel comfortable. Unfortunately, we don't always have the luxury of choice and if forced into an inappropriate learning experience we can feel very anxious.

Many years ago I had the opportunity of attending a two-day management course. It was a very full two days, involving teamwork and problem-solving. We were thrown in at the deep end and given group tasks to accomplish, including building models, designing promotional materials and making presentations. I was terrified and hated every single second I was there and know I learned very little. What I didn't know then was that this method of learning was the worst possible learning scenario for me.

Kolb's learning cycle (Figure 3.1) gives us an insight into why some learning experiences appeal to us and why some can make us feel very anxious.

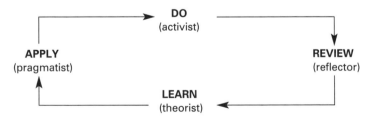

Figure 3.1 Kolb's learning cycle (after Petty, 2004)

There are four stages to learning and we engage in all four of them during the learning process. Some stages of the learning cycle can feel more comfortable to us and some can make us feel uncomfortable or anxious. For example, many learners who are natural reflectors often feel uncomfortable being asked to think on their feet. This is how Clare feels.

CASE STUDY – CLARE

When I was at school I found it very difficult to speak in front of the rest of the class because I hated, and still hate, being put on the spot and knowing that people are looking at me. Even now, I dread my company's training days; I'm terrified that I'll be picked on to say something and everyone will be watching as I make a complete fool of myself.

Supporting learners

We can see from Clare's experience how easy it is for us to place learners in situations that can cause them anxiety. Of course, we won't know the individual preferences of all our learners, at least not until we know them well. Nor can we always avoid, or indeed, want to avoid, every situation that might make a learner feel a little uncomfortable. But some learners will be very anxious about language and literacy and we do need to be sensitive to their anxieties.

You might think that the experience of developing language and literacy skills is no different from learning about hairdressing or accountancy or even numeracy for that matter. Not so. We saw earlier in this chapter how our language is part of our identity. Unlike other subjects, language and literacy learning is personal. It's not just learning about a subject, it's about who we are and when we fail it's a very personal failure.

There is more. Our success or failure in language and literacy is visible. Unlike our knowledge of, say computers or geography, unless we are keen on pub quizzes, it's unlikely that other people will know about our weaknesses. But language and literacy skills are public property; people we know and meet in daily life will certainly know how effective we are at verbal communication and many will have an idea of our level of competence in literacy. Read what Geoff has to say.

CASE STUDY – GEOFF

I've always managed to get by with my writing but it's not something I'm very good at. I have to be really careful when I write so that it's not obvious that it's a weak area for me. It's funny but, you know, I've often heard people say they are no good at maths – as soon as one person says it everyone else joins in – it's almost a competition for who is the worst. Yet I've never heard anyone say they're no good at writing and I've always kept quiet about my problems. You know, I would like to write really well but the only courses I know about are those basic literacy things and I'm certainly not that bad.

Geoff's experience shows us just how personal our language and literacy skills are, and that learners sometimes need to work hard to prevent those around them from discovering their weaknesses.

We have looked at some of the many and varied factors that influence language and literacy development and affect a learner's skills, attitudes and motivation. We know that each learner will have a unique profile in terms of experience, skills, attitude, motivation and preferred style of learning. We can support them by tapping into this knowledge and providing experiences of language and literacy that play to their strengths and allow them to experience success. But how do we know their individual strengths? The answer lies in getting to know our learners, finding time in our busy schedules to talk to them and importantly, to listen when they talk to us. We will return to this theme in later chapters.

A SUMMARY OF KEY POINTS

> Children appear to have an innate capacity for language learning which is developed by exposure to language, positive reinforcement and cognitive ability.

> The way we use language is an essential part of our identity; each of us has a personal experience of language influenced by factors such as our socio-economic status, gender, peer group and ethnicity.

> Motivation for developing language and literacy skills can be personal or instrumental.

> Labelling and stereotyping can influence a learner's own perception of their language and literacy skills.

> Previous experience will affect the attitudes that learners will have to language and literacy; confidence can be severely undermined by negative experiences at school.

> Language and literacy skills should be developed within a meaningful context to enable learners to see their relevance.

> We need to be aware that learners can have a variety of anxieties connected with language and literacy.

Branching options

The following tasks are designed to help you consolidate and develop your understanding of the factors affecting the acquisition and development of language and literacy skills.

Reflection

Are there any critical experiences within your own learning which motivated you to read or write about a particular subject? Consider how this experience might in some way be integrated into your own teaching, and note this in your journal for future reference.

Analysis

Identify a learner in one of your classes who is well motivated to learn the subject but who appears anxious about reading or writing. What strategies could you use to overcome this? Note these and any progress you make in your journal.

Research

What aspects of the theories described in this chapter do you feel are relevant to developing the literacy skills of your learners? Use the references to research these aspects in more detail, and identify any changes in your planning strategies that you will employ in future lessons.

REFERENCES AND FURTHER READING REFERENCES AND FURTHER READING

Bernstein, B (1975) *Class, codes and control*. London: Routledge and Kegan Paul.
Child, D (1993) *Psychology and the teacher*. London: Cassell.
Cole, M (1989) *Education for equality*. London: RoutledgeFalmer.
Fromkin, V, Rodman, R and Hyams, R (2003) *An introduction to language.* Boston, MA: Thomson Heinle.
Lowe, M and Graham, B (1998) *English language for beginners.* London: Writers and Readers.
Milroy, L (1987) Social network and language maintenance, in Mayor B and Pugh A K (ed) *Language, communication and education.* Beckenham: Croom Helm.
Nichols, P (1987) Women in their speech communities, O'Barr, W and Atkins, B (1987) Women's language or powerless language?, in Mayor B and Pugh A K (ed) *Language, communication and education.* Beckenham: Croom Helm.
Petty, G (2001) *Teaching today*. Cheltenham: Nelson Thornes.
Rogers, C (1983) *Freedom to learn for the 80s*. New York: Macmillan.
Rogers, J (2007*) Adults learning*. Maidenhead: Open University Press.
Shaw, J (1995) *Education, gender and anxiety*. London: Taylor and Francis.

4
Participation

This chapter will help you to:

- **consider the importance of language and literacy skills in enabling learners to participate fully in life.**

Links to minimum core elements:

A 1.1   The different factors affecting the acquisition and development of language and literacy skills.

A 1.2   The importance of English language and literacy in enabling users to participate in public life, society and the modern economy.

A 1.3   Potential barriers that can hinder development of language skills.

A 1.4   The main learning disabilities and difficulties relating to language learning and skill development.

Links to LLUK Professional Standards for QTLS:
AS3, AS4, AS7, AK3.1, AP3.1, AK4.1, AP4.1, BK2.2, BP2.2, BK2.3, BP2.3, BK3.1, BK3.2, BK3.3, BK3.4, BP3.1, BP3.2, BP3.3, BP3.4, CK3.3, CK3.4, CP3.3, CP3.4.

Links to LLUK mandatory units of assessment:
Planning and enabling learning (CTLLS and DTLLS):

- **understand how to plan for inclusive learning;**
- **understand how to use teaching and learning strategies and resources inclusively to meet curriculum requirements;**
- **understand and demonstrate knowledge of the minimum core in own practice.**

Theories and principles for planning and enabling learning (DTLLS):

- **understand the application of theories and principles of learning and communication to inclusive practice;**
- **understand how to apply theories and principles of learning and communication in planning and enabling inclusive learning;**
- **understand and demonstrate knowledge of the minimum core in own practice.**

Introduction

We encourage learners to believe that they can achieve their learning goals and, provided these are realistic, it is right and proper that we should do so. But with just a moment's thought we realise that sometimes learners will not achieve their goals because their language and literacy skills are limited. We also know that there are numerous doors that open only with the keys of good language and literacy skills: doors into careers and into participating in public and social life. If we don't have the keys some doors will just not budge. In this chapter we will explore the role of language and literacy in opening doors and determining life choices. We will look at how these choices affect the individual and consider some strategies we can use to support learners.

Literacy and life choices

REFLECTIVE TASK

REFLECTIVE TASK

Consider examples of how your use of English has either opened or closed a door for you. Some examples might include being excluded from a friendship group as a child because you had a different accent or being asked to contribute to your firm's magazine because you are an imaginative writer.

We will follow the example of Charles Dickens's David Copperfield and start at the beginning: we will look at what happens when children begin formal education. In the previous chapter, Bernstein's work (1975) on language development showed us the relationship between socio-economic groups and restricted and elaborated language codes. Bernstein believed that a restricted language code clashed with the academic culture found in school. Children with a restricted code can find the school environment difficult to deal with and this can compromise their achievement levels.

Bernstein's work gives us some insight into the relationship between language skills and educational achievement. Obviously, other factors are involved, but the link between language and achievement and therefore between language and level of qualification has been made. There are also other important factors of language that can impact on achievement, for example autistic spectrum disorder or dyslexia. Gaining an academic qualification becomes problematic if you struggle with the methods or vehicles of assessment. This is important because qualifications almost always dictate access to employment.

Here, Paul and Bethan talk about school, educational achievement and life choices. Paul is describing his experience of coping with dyslexia.

CASE STUDY – PAUL

I struggled with English at school. I refused to read out loud for teachers as the rest of the class laughed at me and made fun of my pronunciation, and teachers also got mad with me for my slow reading. Always got frustrated as everyone else was better than me and could spell. I ended up in the remedial group. I used to come top so eventually they moved me into a higher group where I was classed as thick and so made to sit at the back doing other work. I never learnt anything, most of the time played cards.

I wasn't allowed to take English O level, just took CSE language. They also made me take history when I wanted to take art. Got good grades in metalwork, woodwork and technical drawing. On my reports the teachers always said I could do better but never said how. I always wanted to be a draughtsman but was told I would never be good enough at maths and English. I had to find a job where you could use your hands and not your head so I became an apprentice at an electrical rewind company when I left school.

Bethan describes her difficulties in coping with the academic culture of the school.

> ## CASE STUDY – BETHAN
>
> *I hated school. I just didn't want to be there so I couldn't be bothered to do any work. Actually, no – it was more I couldn't do it – well, I could do it but it all seemed to be such an effort. I had loads of different jobs after I left school, then I met Mark and now we've got the kids. I'm the main breadwinner because it's much easier for me to get work than Mark but it's all part-time and I only ever get the minimum. Mark does most of the stuff around the house, when he's here that is – we're always rowing and he often gets fed up and goes back to his mum's for a while.*

On leaving school both Paul and Bethan found a limited choice of available career options. This is a wasted opportunity for the individual. But it is just as much a waste for society. New technology, for example, requires high levels of language and literacy skills.

> *In so many aspects of our life we still need to read, a need technology cannot replace. Indeed in some ways it makes it more essential. As more everyday activities become automated, so reading becomes more important.*
>
> (DfES, 2001, p54)

Good communication skills are perhaps even more important in the service industries.

> *Speaking and listening is by far the most widespread form of communication even in the most literate person's life. In most jobs people spend much more time speaking, listening and discussing than reading or writing.*
>
> (DfES, 2001, p20)

The effects of limited language and literacy skills on the individual

We have established a link between limited language and literacy skills and career choice. Let's take this a little further and explore two of the less obvious, but equally important, consequences of compromised language and literacy skills: low self-esteem and social exclusion.

Self-esteem

> *For some the continual pressure of learning to cope with their literacy weakness can result in enormous stress. So what began a long time ago in school as an educational problem gradually becomes a social and emotional problem. With regular failure in a skill that society values, people eventually lose confidence in themselves generally. It should come as no surprise to discover that there is an association between literacy skills and self-esteem. People who have low attainments in literacy usually have lower self-esteem than the rest of us.*
>
> (Lawrence, 2000, Introduction)

Paul and Bethan talk again about their experiences and about how they feel about themselves. Paul received little support at school for his dyslexia and clearly suffered as a result.

> ## CASE STUDY – PAUL AND BETHAN
>
> *I always classed myself as thick so I was never motivated to read or do any other qualifications. Found I was good with my hands so worked on that. I just accepted I was too thick for anything else. Luckily I met my wife and she pushed me into changing direction. I passed my electrical qualifications and now I assess NVQ students in a Further Education college. I still struggle with my confidence especially when it comes to writing. People see me as confident and capable, I don't feel it. I think I need to put extra effort in to be the confident person.*
>
> Bethan also struggles with self-confidence.
>
> *Do you remember that woman on the TV who used to make up those silly poems – I think her name was Pam something. There was this poem called,* Oh I wish I'd looked after me teeth. *Well my poem would be* Oh I wish I'd worked harder at school. *I really do. I still get panicky when I have to fill in a form – I put it off until the last moment. It does get me down sometimes. I think I'm not good enough, not good enough to help the kids with their schoolwork and well – just not good enough as a person.*

Paul and Bethan's experiences have had a huge impact on their self-esteem. With support from his wife, Paul was able to gain the qualifications that opened up new career opportunities, although you can see that, despite a satisfying and rewarding job, Paul still feels that he has to work to maintain his confidence levels and self-esteem. Bethan hasn't yet been able to take the same steps as Paul. Why is this? In the following section we will look at some possible explanations.

Social exclusion

> Social exclusion can happen when individuals or areas suffer from a combination of linked problems such as unemployment, poor skills, low incomes, poor housing, high crime environments, bad health and family breakdown.
>
> (Marsh, 1999, p2)

We will make a final visit to Bethan; this time she describes how her life as a whole is affected by her limited literacy skills.

> ## CASE STUDY – BETHAN
>
> *Sometimes it is a struggle – the kids are great, but you know it's hard when you have to keep saying No, we can't afford it. And I know they miss their dad when he goes off in a huff to his mum's. I also worry that they will get into trouble when they're bigger because lots of kids round here do. There's nothing for them to do here – it's no wonder they get bored. And we hardly ever go anywhere or do nice fun things with the kids like going to the leisure centre because it all costs too much. That's the way things are isn't it – it's no good moaning and I'm better off than lots of people.*

There are a number of important points we can draw from Bethan's comments. The first is that her children are also affected. Indeed, as Millar (1993) points out, the knock-on effects of poor literacy skills involve the whole family and the whole family suffers.

Bethan's comments also reveal how the family has become marginalised or socially excluded; they are not able to participate in the normal activities nor do they have access to support networks that most of us take for granted.

Social exclusion is more than just income poverty – it is a lack of access to the networks of support and information that help people into education, homes, jobs, services and appropriate benefits.

(DEMOS, 1997, p1)

PRACTICAL TASK PRACTICAL TASK PRACTICAL TASK PRACTICAL TASK PRACTICAL TASK

Can you identify any other examples of social exclusion that Bethan's family is vulnerable to?

You may have thought of the following.

- Education: Bethan and her husband, Mark, might feel anxious about joining a learning programme. They might also find it difficult to discuss their children's educational needs with the school or to participate in organisations such as the Parent–Teachers' Association.
- Health: Bethan and Mark might not have confidence in their use of assertive language to talk to health professionals.
- Citizens' rights: the family is vulnerable because it does not have access to knowledge of public and civil rights.

There is another side to social exclusion. Bethan is pessimistic about any possibility for change and has accepted the status quo. Despite her desire for an education she will struggle to take it any further unless she can gain confidence and self-esteem. Even then, the memories she has of failing at school may be too powerful to overcome. If you have already failed at school, why risk it again? (Evans, 2003) But let us suppose for a moment that Bethan does manage to take that step. What would her experience of returning to education as an adult be if she walked into your class? And what can we do to support her and similar potential learners?

Supporting learners

REFLECTIVE TASK

Imagine you have just arrived in a foreign country where you do not speak the language. You are in the Arrivals section of the airport. The building is strange; you don't know where you must go. You can't read the signs, nor can you understand what people are saying to you. How would you feel?

You may have identified feelings of fear, frustration, disorientation, anger or helplessness. This is an extreme analogy, but it does give an indication of how nerve-racking and frustrating it can be when learners with limited language and literacy skills enter education as adults.

If you teach an academic subject, for example psychology or maths, you may well have transferred effortlessly from school to college and/or university and then into teaching. But perhaps your teaching subject is more vocational – accountancy, computers or plumbing – and you returned to education as an adult, either from industry or, like me, after caring for children. If so, you may well remember that very first step you took back into education; this step might even have been as recent as beginning your teacher training programme. Can you recall how you felt at the point of your first experience in an educational institution as an adult? I certainly can; I remember feeling extremely anxious; so anxious that I circled the college building before I felt able to enter.

Anxiety is a fairly common feeling experienced by adults on re-entering education, even for adults who have good language skills. But for those with limited skills, with low self-esteem and little self-confidence, undertaking any programme of study or even entering an educational institution can be daunting. To help us understand the relationship between a learner's self-esteem and motivation we are going to look at Maslow's hierarchy of needs model and then at psychologist Denis Lawrence's work (2000) on literacy and self-esteem.

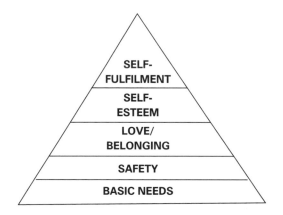

Figure 4.1 A hierarchy of needs (based on Maslow, 1970)

You are probably familiar with Maslow's model (Figure 4.1), so this is just a brief reminder of how it works. The lowest, or initial level of the model includes basic physical human needs such as food and water; the highest, or final level, self-fulfilment is where we are able to attain our full potential. As each level of need is satisfied we are able to consider moving to the next level. For our purposes we need only be concerned with level four, self-esteem. Maslow identified two esteem needs: we need to believe in our own competence and we need recognition from others. If these needs are missing we can struggle to make changes that could offer more fulfilling experiences.

We saw from Bethan's story that she felt inferior and helpless; she had little self-belief and there is no indication that she received recognition from those around her. She wasn't able to consider making positive changes because of her unmet needs. Bethan had a desire for self-fulfilment, *I wish I'd worked harder at school, I really do*, but was unable to take it further.

Learners need to believe in themselves and to feel that others recognise their abilities before they gain confidence and motivation. The trick for us is to recognise their fears and insecurities. So how do we identify the signals? And once we have identified them, what do we do about it?

Make a list of the ways you think a learner might signal feelings of anxiety and insecurity. Compare your list with the comments in the following paragraph.

Lawrence (2000) offers some guidance for us here. He suggests that people with low self-esteem react to their literacy difficulties in one of two ways: they will withdraw or they will feel angry. In the classroom learners who withdraw might appear nervous or timid about undertaking a task that they would see as stressful. They might be reluctant to participate in a class discussion or volunteer to answer questions through fear of saying the wrong thing. They might make excuses for their behaviour; they might, for example, say they have no time to do homework. A learner who is feeling angry might appear boastful or arrogant, or they might blame others in order to boost their self-esteem. Alternatively, they might appear bored and uninterested in a task or topic.

Grace, who is working towards a CTLLS qualification, had to deal with a situation like this. Here is an extract from her journal.

CASE STUDY – GRACE

I feel I really achieved something yesterday because I managed to turn around something that has been worrying me. One of women on the First Aid in the Workplace course, I'll call her L, seemed to be totally uninterested in anything we have been doing and spent most of each session since the programme started three weeks ago, with a permanent scowl on her face. To be honest, I took it personally, thinking she was bored at the way I was teaching. I'd tried to involve her more but hadn't succeeded. Then, after last week's class, I had to stay on in town and had a spare hour, so I went into the cafe next door and she was there, on her own, having a coffee. My heart sank and I was tempted to go and sit at another table, but instead I asked her if I could join her. I'm so pleased that I did because we got talking and she confided to me that she spends most of each session terrified that I'll ask her something and she'll have to talk in front of everyone. I had no idea. She then said she felt a lot happier just telling me her concerns and felt I'd really listened to her. Then yesterday, I was careful to draw her in gently by asking her a couple of straightforward, short answer questions that she was able to answer without too much stress and I could see she felt more confident because her scowl had disappeared.

Grace was able to resolve her problem through a chance meeting that gave her insight into L's behaviour. Lawrence offers us some guidance for how we can help learners, such as L, with low self-esteem. Clearly writing from a humanist viewpoint, he suggests that the human qualities of acceptance, genuineness and empathy are essential in a teacher who desires to enhance a learner's self-esteem. These qualities have a number of beneficial outcomes. Firstly, an environment where acceptance, genuineness and empathy are the norm is a non-threatening one. Within it, learners are able to gain confidence. In turn, this will increase their self-esteem and motivation. Secondly, this environment is one that enables us to become better communicators. Thirdly, we are able to provide a model for our learners to copy.

It is worth looking a little closer at what is meant by acceptance, genuineness and empathy. Lawrence tells us that acceptance means *being able to accept the person unconditionally even if you disagree with their views, or even with their behaviour*

(Lawrence, 2000, p42). Equally important is being able to *show* our acceptance. This is not always easy and, in fact, poses a problem for us. If someone expresses views that are radically different from ours we might try to convey acceptance but, if we don't honestly feel it, our non-verbal signals can indicate our true feelings. Lawrence suggests that the solution to this problem lies with us; it lies, in fact, with our own level of self-confidence. Again, this is not easy because we don't necessarily feel confident. This is especially true in the early weeks and months of our teaching career. However, if we are able show learners that we can see their point of view and that we understand how they feel, in other words showing empathy, this can only help to increase our own confidence. Good listening skills and an awareness of our non-verbal signals are important in developing skills in empathy. We will explore both these aspects in detail in Chapter 7, Speaking and Listening, and in Chapter 8, Non-verbal Communication.

So far we have been looking at the experiences of learners with clear difficulties in language and literacy. The majority of these learners will already be receiving support, their difficulties having been identified during initial assessment. But all learners need to develop their literacy skills, not only to gain their qualification but, as we have already seen, to open numerous doors. And they can do it, with our support, within their subject learning.

Having said this, all learners' language and literacy needs are not going to be the same. Nor should we assume that overall an individual learner will have an even level of need. The reason for this, as we saw in the previous chapter, is that each of us has our own personal language identity. This inevitably means that our experience and understanding of it will be unique to us. What is perhaps less obvious is that each of us is likely have an uneven profile, or level of competency. We may in fact be a good verbal communicator but find writing more difficult; we may read well but struggle with some of the finer points of punctuation. This unevenness is referred to as a *spiky profile.* My own spiky profile reveals a weakness in spelling; there are certain words that still defeat me. You, too, will have a spiky profile (identified in the skills audit you completed in Chapter 2).

Sometimes the spiky profile a learner presents can take you by surprise. Sandra was one of my very first learners. We were working in a small group on communication skills on a *Return to Learn* programme. Sandra found it extremely difficult to speak in front of a group of people. However, Sandra was well qualified academically; indeed she had a PhD, so was very able in her reading, writing and listening skills but she struggled painfully with speaking in front of others. So, if a learner appears to be confident in one area of language and literacy it doesn't necessarily follow that they are equally confident in all areas.

In the previous chapter we saw how important it is for us to get to know our learners so that we can offer them learning experiences that play to their strengths. The same applies here. If we can find time to talk and listen to learners and to be receptive to their non-verbal and behavioural signals we will very soon learn to recognise when they are feeling anxious or frustrated.

We know that our learners will need to have high levels of language and literacy skills to enable them to participate fully in public and social life. By giving them the opportunity to develop their language and literacy skills within their subject learning we are increasing the choices they will have at their disposal.

A SUMMARY OF KEY POINTS

> There is a relationship between language, literacy and life choices.

> Language and literacy play an important role in enabling people to participate in normal social activities.

> Limited language and literacy skills can indirectly lead to social exclusion.

> Adults with poor language and literacy skills often have low self-confidence and self-esteem.

> Acceptance, genuineness and empathy can help learners with poor language and literacy skills to build self-esteem and gain motivation.

Branching options

The following tasks are designed to help you consolidate and develop your understanding of the importance of English language and literacy in enabling users to participate in public life, society and the modern economy.

Reflection

Think of an experience in which you had difficulty in understanding language. Perhaps this would be a visit to Europe on holiday when you were unable to ask for directions or join in a conversation. How did this experience affect your confidence and your subsequent approach to similar situations? Note in your journal how this may be relevant to understanding your learners' language problems.

Analysis

Consider again the learner that you identified in the previous chapter who was anxious about reading or writing. What was the cause of this anxiety? To what extent do you think they could be socially excluded, and how do you think this might affect their approach to participating in learning?

Research

Do you agree with Lawrence's humanist approach to building self-esteem with learners? How can his approach help you to deal with learners with language and literacy problems?

REFERENCES AND FURTHER READING REFERENCES AND FURTHER READING

Aldridge, F and Tuckett, A (2001) *Survey of adult participation in learning.* Leicester: NIACE.

Bernstein, B (1975) *Class, codes and control.* London: Routledge and Kegan Paul.

Child, D (1993) *Psychology and the teacher.* London: Cassell.

DEMOS (1997) *The wealth and poverty of networks.* London: DEMOS.

DfES (2001) *Adult Literacy Core Curriculum.* London: DfES.

Evans, N (2003) *Making sense of lifelong learning.* London: Routledge.

Lawrence, D (2000) *Building self-esteem with adult learners.* London: Paul Chapman Publishing.

Marsh, A (1999) Housing and health. *Radical Statistics Journal*, 72.

Maslow, A. (1970) *Motivation and Personality*, 2nd edn. New York: Harper.

Millar, J (1993) The continuing trend in rising poverty. In Sinfield, A (ed) *Poverty, inequality and justice.* Edinburgh: Edinburgh University Press.

5
Barriers

This chapter will help you to:

- **understand some of the barriers to language and literacy development.**

Links to minimum core elements:

A 1.1   The different factors affecting the acquisition and development of language and literacy skills.

A 1.2   The importance of English language and literacy in enabling users to participate in public life, society and the modern economy.

A 1.3   Potential barriers that can hinder development of language skills.

A 1.4   The main learning disabilities and difficulties relating to language learning and skill development.

Links to LLUK Professional Standards for QTLS:
AS3, AS4, AS7, AK3.1, AP3.1, AK4.1, AP4.1, AK5.1, BK2.2, BP2.2, BK2.3, BP2.3, BK3.1, BK3.2, BK3.3, BK3.4, BK3.5, BP3.1, BP3.2, BP3.3, BP3.4, BP3.5, CK3.3, CK3.4, CP3.3, CP3.4.

Links to LLUK mandatory units of assessment:
Planning and enabling learning (CTLLS and DTLLS):
- **understand how to plan for inclusive learning;**
- **understand how to use teaching and learning strategies and resources inclusively to meet curriculum requirements;**
- **understand and demonstrate knowledge of the minimum core in own practice.**

Theories and principles for planning and enabling learning (DTLLS):
- **understand the application of theories and principles of learning and communication to inclusive practice;**
- **understand how to apply theories and principles of learning and communication in planning and enabling inclusive learning;**
- **understand and demonstrate knowledge of the minimum core in own practice.**

Introduction

When learners arrive in the classroom they don't come empty handed; they bring with them attitudes, beliefs, perceptions, expectations, anxieties and problems. Any of these could be a barrier to language and literacy development; indeed may have already prevented some potential learners from making it to the classroom. When those that make it arrive, they have to deal with barriers that exist within the educational environment.

In this chapter we will explore some of the personal, cultural, institutional and organisational barriers that can hinder language and literacy development; we will look at some specific difficulties and disabilities and explore a range of strategies that we can use to minimise barriers and to support learners.

Personal barriers

In the previous chapter we explored the link between language, literacy and educational achievement. We looked at how poor achievers are more vulnerable to poverty and social exclusion. We also saw how social exclusion can lower self-confidence and self-esteem and explored strategies we can use in the classroom to help learners. However, there are other potential personal barriers that can hinder development of language and literacy.

PRACTICAL TASK PRACTICAL TASK PRACTICAL TASK PRACTICAL TASK PRACTICAL TASK

Read Adam's story and make a list of the barriers that prevented him from developing his language and literacy skills.

SCENARIO STUDY – ADAM'S DILEMMA

Adam is in a dilemma. He's fed up with his job but every time he tries to work out how he can change things he comes up against a brick wall. He knows that he could get a better job if he had some qualifications. The trouble is, he is honest enough with himself to know that he really doesn't want the bother. Besides, he can't see how he can get qualifications anyway. For a start, he doesn't know what sort of qualifications he needs and he doesn't know who can advise him. Then there's the problem of attending a course. The nearest college is in the next town, 12 miles away, and with petrol being so expensive it's going to make a hole in his budget. Money is already tight with having to pay his mortgage and money to his ex-wife for the children. But it's not just the money. To be honest, after a long day at work, all he wants to do when he gets home is watch TV, not do a 24-mile round trip on a cold night. And what if he did make the effort? Most likely he'd find himself sitting in a classroom with someone like Killer Blake, his old English teacher, an expert in humiliation techniques, standing in front of him. Now that wouldn't bear thinking about.

Adam's barriers include lack of time, money and information, lack of motivation and unhappy memories of school. Some other personal barriers might include inconvenient timetabling, lack of appropriate courses, family responsibilities, health problems, the perception that learning is unnecessary or not relevant, lack of confidence, anxiety and low self-esteem.

Some learners have additional personal difficulties or disabilities that can hinder their development of language and literacy skills. Here, two learners talk about their experiences of learning. Maggie is partially sighted.

CASE STUDY – MAGGIE

I lost the sight in my left eye about three years ago after an accident. I manage well most of the time, especially when the teacher is talking to the whole class but when we are working in groups I have to angle it so that I always sit where everyone else is in view of my good eye. I try to do it without them realising because I don't like to keep asking, Can I sit in that seat because it's the only one where I can see you all?

Bob has difficulty with hearing.

CASE STUDY – BOB

I have hearing problems. It's probably my own fault. I worked for years in the motor repair industry. There was always a lot of noise and I wasn't always careful enough to wear protection. My problem now is being able to hear words clearly. I've got a hearing aid but it amplifies everything, including background noise. I can hear people but I can't always pick out the words. I can hear some of the words so I can work out a lot of what people are saying using a bit of lip-reading to fill in the gaps, but it takes me a few seconds and everyone is on to the next thing by then. I think the rest of the class probably gets fed up waiting for me to catch up. I get very frustrated and embarrassed.

Maggie and Bob are anxious not to stand out in the class as being different. We can understand their feelings. We know that we make judgements about others on first impressions. When someone is different it can sometimes make us feel uncomfortable. There is a chance that Maggie and Bob could become isolated from the rest of the group; they are already at risk because their difficulties affect their communication skills.

Cultural and institutional barriers

When we talk about cultural and institutional factors we are referring to the influences society and the institutions within it, such as the family or education, have on us as individuals. A useful starting point for exploring cultural barriers to language and literacy development is to look at some of the cultural expectations that families, peer groups and ethnic groups may have of their members.

It isn't that unusual for people to encounter puzzlement or even disapproval from those around them when they choose to undertake voluntary education, an activity that is sometimes viewed as middle class (McGivney, 1993). Meg talks here about the attitudes of those around her when she considered returning to education as an adult.

CASE STUDY – MEG

I wanted that English GCE; I don't think my friends and family knew how much I wanted it. My dad said, Don't waste your time going to that evening class. What's the point anyway? You've got a job. My friends said, We're going dancing, come with us. That was 15 years ago. I had the last laugh though. Getting that one qualification made such a difference to me; it gave me so much confidence. I thought, if I can get one, I can get more. And I did. I kept going until I got a degree. At the time though, it was very hard for me to do something that everyone around me thought was totally pointless.

So have things changed since Meg's experience? Not all that much it seems:

In our country today, far too many people are still locked in a culture that regards lifelong learning as either unnecessary, unappealing, uninteresting or unavailable. Once schooling or immediate post-school education is over, they want nothing more of learning than it should largely leave them alone.
    (NAGCELL, 1999, *Creating learning cultures*, para. 3.6, cited in Evans, 2003, p70)

Cultural expectations can influence a whole generation of people. One particularly vulnerable group is that of older, retired people. Evans (2003) calls this group *an increasingly significant category of the missing* (from learning). The erroneous cultural stereotype that *you can't teach an old dog new tricks* persists sufficiently to persuade numerous older people that it is a truth.

For learners whose previous education took place outside the UK the cultural barriers are substantial. Do you remember Hai Ling who talked, in Chapter 3, about her experiences of learning English? Here she talks about the difficulties she faced in adapting to UK teaching and learning approaches.

CASE STUDY – HAI LING

In China the teachers stand out in front of the class and talk, sometimes with a microphone as classes are very big. It is very disciplined. The students have to listen, make notes and answer questions. There are a lot of tests and exams. Also, the students rarely challenge the teacher. Education in the UK is completely different from China. The first thing I noticed here was that students have to take part in discussions; this is quite hard for us because we are not used to it.

PRACTICAL TASK PRACTICAL TASK PRACTICAL TASK PRACTICAL TASK PRACTICAL TASK

We have looked at how society can stereotype older people and the cultural barriers faced by ethnic groups. Can you identify any other groups vulnerable to cultural influences?

You could have thought of teenagers who may be influenced by friends, people with disabilities or those within a family that views education as meaningless. McGivney (1993) notes that family members can sometimes be hostile. They may not understand what is happening, and can feel excluded when their partner becomes interested in studying. You may remember the scene in *Educating Rita* where Rita's husband burns her textbooks to prevent her from studying.

Organisational barriers

There are many potential barriers that can exist within educational organisations. Let's look at a few.

Language barriers

During the research for this book I carried out a brief survey, with a group of 45 people, on how literacy is perceived. I wrote the word *literacy* in large letters on an even larger sheet of paper and pinned it to the wall. I then asked everyone to write down their immediate gut feelings on seeing the word.

REFLECTIVE TASK
REFLECTIVE TASK

What are your immediate feelings about the word *literacy*?

You may have identified both positive and negative feelings, but if they were mainly negative you are in good company; the majority of responses from the 45 people who took part in my research were also negative. Indeed, once I had filtered out the neutral responses (mainly definitions) there were 31 negative and 9 positive responses.

You might be interested to know what these were. The positive responses were: interesting, relevant, purposeful, content, delightful, enthusiastic, happiness, enjoyment (mentioned twice). The negative responses were: frustrated, stupid, confused, scary (mentioned twice), complicated, hard to understand, boring (mentioned three times), difficult (mentioned twice), uninterested, not creative, extra work, exams and testing (mentioned seven times), bad word, I can't spell, help (mentioned twice), stress, pressure, fear (mentioned twice) and terror. So, who were the guinea pigs that they should have such a strong negative reaction to the word literacy? Not, as you might expect, people struggling with literacy. But, you've probably guessed, they were all on initial teacher training programmes.

This small survey gives an indication of the potency of language, how one simple word can conjure up such strong responses. And we can see how discouraging it could be for learners when faced with a slot on their timetable entitled *literacy*. Literacy is an academic word, bandied around comfortably in an academic environment, but not a word you'd hear too often elsewhere. And it's not the only one. Educational organisations, where we train and work, are littered with them: *outcomes*, *validation*, *curriculum*. And how about *minimum core*? Clearly, educational language can be a huge barrier for some learners. We need to be aware of this, especially at the start of new programmes when learners can already be feeling anxious. Do we take time to explain carefully the meaning of specialised words, or do we just assume that learners will understand?

PRACTICAL TASK PRACTICAL TASK PRACTICAL TASK PRACTICAL TASK PRACTICAL TASK

List some of the specialised words used within your organisation or subject area, and note in your journal how you could introduce them to your learners.

Here is another word that has the potential to turn learners off: *assessment*. For many, the fear of being assessed on their performance is strong enough to make a difference. Mary, who has been teaching a painting class for a number of years, tells the story of the demise of her daytime group.

CASE STUDY – MARY

Many of my students have been with me for a long time. Some of them are elderly and widowed, so they really look forward to coming, and have produced some good work over the years. We've now been told that we can't continue the classes unless I introduce assessment. Everyone is upset about it, and frightened; assessment is the last thing on their minds, they just want to learn more about painting, to improve their skills and enjoy their morning. They have decided they don't want to continue, so I won't be running a daytime course next term.

Practical/communication barriers

A number of the more practical elements of learning, such as the timetabling of programmes and the degree of physical comfort on offer, can also be a barrier. Is there sufficient lighting in the classroom? Is it warm enough on bitter January evenings? Is there somewhere for the learners to enjoy a coffee break? Most importantly, is there a good communication system in place? Unfortunately, some organisational barriers, such as timetabling, are probably beyond our control. Indeed, sometimes we do our very best to meet our learners' needs but still find ourselves caught out, as the following comments from Tony show.

CASE STUDY – TONY

It was the first session of a Spanish course and there were about eight of us waiting outside the building. The teacher had gone to see if she could find anyone to open the door for us. After about ten minutes she returned, embarrassed to tell us that, although she had arranged that morning for the key holder to open up the building, there must have been a breakdown somewhere. She apologised profusely and we all agreed to return the following week. Would you believe it, the next week was a repeat performance, no key holder. The teacher was so mortified that she took all of us to her home and we sat round her kitchen table.

Another potential barrier is the availability of access to support services. In larger organisations, such as colleges and public services training, there is usually good access to a comprehensive support system that normally includes education and career advisers, counsellors and welfare advisers. Not so in small set-ups. Very often you, the teacher, will be out on a limb and will need to think of alternative ways of providing your learners with access to appropriate advisers.

PRACTICAL TASK PRACTICAL TASK PRACTICAL TASK PRACTICAL TASK PRACTICAL TASK

Identify the referral systems within your organisation. List them in your journal and identify how they could be used to support your learners.

Minimising barriers and supporting learners

One question that I always included in course evaluations for community education programmes was, *What have you liked most about this course*? One response to this question, *the social aspect of learning*, appeared in one form or another probably more than any other. This sometimes made me wonder whether, without it, some learners would have dropped out of the programme. I don't know; I never asked, but I suspect that it might have been true for some. It's possible then that a major reason some learners attend and complete programmes is that learning offers an opportunity to socialise with others who are sharing the experience:

... the social side of learning should never be underestimated. Meeting people who share a common purpose is something that many if not most people enjoy doing ... For many present-day participants it is the social aspect of learning which appeals so strongly.

(Evans, 2003, p120)

There are limits of course to the degree to which we can offer the social element. Coffee-shop style sofas and easy chairs would be very nice but we have little control over the nature and comfort of the facilities in our organisation. Yet, we can create the sort of environment that facilitates social interaction by offering opportunities during sessions for learners to talk to each other and by providing the all-important coffee break. But one of the most valuable things we can do is very simple. It's about learning names. When learners know each other's names they talk to each other. Of course, your learners might already know each other, but if they don't, at the very start of a programme allow a chunk of time for learning names. This can be incorporated into ice-breaking activities to save some time, but it must be much more than just going around the class asking everyone to say their name and something about themselves.

I have found that the following activity works well.

1 Give everyone a large name card to hold or to place on the desk in front of them. Names need to be written in large bold letters in the form that each person wishes to be addressed: this is almost invariably first names or shortened first names.
2 Start the ball rolling by choosing a learner and asking them a question, any question, but you set the tone. This learner then replies to your question. The most important part of this interaction is that you say the learner's name clearly when you ask the question and they must say your name when they reply; if they don't, they have to repeat their reply.
3 That learner then chooses someone else and asks a question, and so on. You need to be very strict about saying names every time a question is asked and answered; this is a real ice-breaker because some people forget and, of course, the rest of the group is amused. When everyone feels reasonably confident, you can do away with the name cards, although this might not be until the start of the second session. (This activity has another advantage; it provides you, the teacher, with valuable information about your learners.)

One important task we have is to develop a supportive learning environment. For learners with specific difficulties this means managing group work so that everyone has an opportunity to participate equally. This may mean stepping in and facilitating for a short while, even stopping the flow of conversation to make sure that everyone is equally involved. We want the group as a whole to take responsibility for supporting its members. Our example will offer a model of good practice for the group to adopt.

From the very first contact we have with a learner our task is to dispel, as far as we are able, any barriers as soon as possible. A tall order, you're thinking, and you are right. We won't necessarily be aware of the psychological, practical or physical problems learners have to deal with on a day-to-day basis. Nevertheless, we cannot afford to neglect this aspect of our role. Here are some tried and tested strategies; they should become part of your general teaching repertoire but are especially helpful in supporting learners with specific barriers.

• Find out as much as you can beforehand; it's definitely a good idea to telephone each one to let them know you are looking forward to seeing them. This is just the first step on the road to building a good relationship with them.
• Ice-breakers, such as the naming activity above, are always a good way to break down barriers, especially if they make people laugh. Incorporating some fun activities is an immensely helpful strategy for promoting good communication.
• Give learners plenty of opportunities to be successful and provide lots of encouragement and assurance en route. One good way to do this is to tap into their individual knowledge, interests and enthusiasms.

- Encourage a supportive environment. Learners with specific difficulties need the support of those around them if they are not to lose confidence.
- Don't make generalisations about learners with specific difficulties. Always ask them what they need and remember that they are the experts.
- Try to plan flexible learning programmes to suit a variety of learners' needs.
- Produce written notes in advance.
- Speak clearly, avoiding jargon, explaining tasks carefully and checking understanding.
- Arrange seating so that everyone can see and be seen. Ensure good lighting and try to eliminate background noise.
- Make sure that learners who have missed a session are able to catch up easily.
- Use specialist support staff, if available, and make sure you know the referral systems in your organisation.

Supporting learners with learning difficulties and disabilities

The *Access for All* document (DfES, 2001) was commissioned to support the delivery of literacy and numeracy core curricula. It states that at least eight and a half million people meet the Disability Discrimination Act definition, and it offers some useful guidance for us in supporting learners with a range of learning difficulties and disabilities, including:

- deaf or partially hearing learners;
- blind or partially sighted learners;
- learners with mental health problems;
- learners with dysloxia;
- learners with physical disabilities;
- learners with learning difficulties;
- learners with autistic spectrum disorder.

Deaf or partially hearing learners
Learners can be anywhere along a continuum from only slightly deaf to profoundly deaf. They may communicate using speech, lip-reading, sign language such as BSL, a hearing aid or a combination of these. Sign language sometimes requires a support worker to interpret. Lip-reading relies on clear speech, context, good lighting and acoustics and a quiet environment. Hearing aids amplify sounds but are limited in their effectiveness; for example, they amplify all sounds equally, including background noise.

Blind or partially sighted learners
Learners can be anywhere along a continuum from only slightly affected to completely blind. Some people have difficulty seeing print even if there is nothing wrong with their eyes. A small proportion of blind people will use Braille, or Moon, a simplified tactile system similar to Braille. Most partially sighted people will prefer:

- large print in a clear non-serif font such as Arial;
- black print on white or yellow paper or white print on black paper;
- to use an audio tape or to access information via a personal computer.

Learners with mental health problems
About one in five of us will have mental health problems at some point in our lives. Depression, stress and anxiety are the most common problems and affect levels of confidence and self-esteem. Learners with mental health problems may be taking medication that can affect their concentration, memory and their ability to participate;

they may have good and bad days that can affect their attendance, punctuality and behaviour. They are likely to find literacy, especially assessment activities such as written tests, particularly stressful. This may require them to withdraw from situations that they find especially uncomfortable.

Learners with dyslexia

Dyslexia, described as a difficulty with processing written language, affects at least ten per cent of the population, is often undiagnosed and affects reading, writing and spelling skills. People with dyslexia often have difficulty decoding words, recognising letters or familiar words, sequencing letters and pronouncing multi-syllabic words. They may have poor short-term memory that can affect their ability to remember written or spoken instructions. They may also have difficulty perceiving print accurately as it can appear blurred or may wobble.

Dyslexic learners develop their own strategies for dealing with their difficulties; for example, they use context, identify patterns and make personal connections to remember things. Computers can minimise problems; for many, just using a keyboard can make a difference, although some learners may need reading and/or voice-recognition software. Cassette recorders can also be helpful.

Learners with physical disabilities

Learners with physical disabilities will almost certainly have experienced many barriers to learning and may have missed out on important stages in developing their language and literacy skills. Important things to consider beforehand are physical access, seating arrangements and appropriate teaching and learning materials. Learners with writing difficulties may need a different pen, an adapted keyboard and/or special arrangements for assessment or examinations.

Learners with speech difficulties may find group work challenging as others in the group might find their speech embarrassing. The following can be helpful.

- Initially ask questions that only need a short answer (but not just a yes or no answer).
- Try to avoid guessing what a learner is saying or completing sentences for them: if necessary ask them to repeat what they have said.
- Do not exclude a learner with a speech difficulty from group activities; instead ensure that other learners do not interrupt.

Learners with learning difficulties

Learning difficulties, which can be mild, moderate or severe, might be compounded by the experience of non-inclusive education resulting in feelings of isolation and low expectations. Learners may have spiky profiles, considerable ability in some areas but difficulties in others; they may also have a range of other factors such as physical disability that can affect their learning. Previous experience of failure might make them reluctant to try anything new and they may try to hide what they cannot do. They may also find it difficult to remember or understand abstract concepts. People with learning difficulties often find practical, non-paper-based activities and visual clues such as graphics helpful.

Learners with autistic spectrum disorder

People with autistic spectrum disorder have difficulty with social interaction; they may not understand social and cultural rules, for example, small talk. They interpret language literally and find metaphors, jokes or abstract concepts difficult to understand. They are often more comfortable with fixed routines and may find even small changes distressing. The following can be helpful.

- Use literal and precise language and carefully worded questions.
- Be sensitive to the fact that they might find group work difficult.
- Discuss any changes to routine beforehand.
- Identify a member of staff to whom the learner can go with any concerns.

A SUMMARY OF KEY POINTS

> Personal barriers include lack of time, money or information, family commitments, health problems, previous school experiences, lack of motivation and a perception of learning as not being relevant.

> Cultural barriers include the expectations and attitudes of family and peer group to learning.

> Organisational barriers include academic language, lack of a social element to learning, a poor physical learning environment and a lack of support available to learners.

> Learners educated outside the UK face specific cultural barriers to language and literacy development.

> We can help reduce barriers when we use strategies that help dispel anxiety and plan learning programmes that take account of the variety of learners' specific needs.

> We need to be familiar with appropriate strategies to support learners with learning difficulties and disabilities.

Branching options

The following tasks are designed to help you consolidate and develop your understanding of barriers that can hinder development of language skills.

Reflection

Did your own experience of family and peer group expectations help or hinder the development of your own language and literacy skills? Consider how this experience may influence your own teaching and note this in your journal.

Analysis

Consider your own organisation. Identify any barriers within the organisation that might discourage potential and actual learners who are under-confident about their literacy ability. How could these barriers be reduced or removed?

Research

Select one of the *Access for All* categories of learners with a range of learning difficulties and disabilities and research in more detail how you can develop your language and literacy teaching strategies to meet the specific needs of these learners.

REFERENCES AND FURTHER READING REFERENCES AND FURTHER READING

Aldridge, F and Tuckett, A (2001) *Survey of adult participation in learning.* Leicester: NIACE.
DfES (2001) *Access for All*. London: DfES.
Evans, N (2003) *Making sense of lifelong learning*. London: Routledge.
McGivney, V (1993) Participation and non-participation: a review of the literature. In Edwards, R, Sieminski, S and Zeldin, D (eds) *Adult learners, education and training*. London: Routledge.

6
Multilingualism and language diversity

Introduction

Some of your learners may be multilingual, typically ESOL learners whose mother tongue is not English. This has implications for the way you plan and deliver your teaching. It means acknowledging these learners' language skills and developing approaches that make best use of their first/other languages as they improve their English language skills. Allied to this is the fact that English is itself a diverse language. Inevitably, your learners will demonstrate a wide variety of English. This diversity needs to be acknowledged and valued while extending learners' language and literacy skills. So, in this chapter we will look at multilingualism and the diversity and variety of English. Then we will look at how we can support learners as they develop their English language skills.

Language diversity

Idiolect, dialect and accent

Each of us has our own individual way of speaking or idiolect. A host of interrelated factors, such as our age, neighbourhood, ethnicity, sex and emotional state, will have influenced the way we pronounce our words, the tone of our voice and the vocabulary we use. Our idiolect is closely linked to our identity. When others make judgements about us from the way we speak it affects our own perception of where we fit in. In her autobiography, Julie Walters (2008) recalls how her mother sent her to a convent school so that she could learn to speak *properly*. Her experience at school led her to believe as she grew up that her own natural speaking voice was in some way inferior and therefore, by implication, that she was somehow not good enough.

Each of us also has a dialect, or language of our particular social/regional group. Our dialect includes the way we pronounce words, our vocabulary and grammar. An example of an East Midlands dialect includes the use of the word *while* in place of *until,* so someone from this region might say *I can't come while Tuesday*. There is a story of a Scunthorpe teacher saying to her inattentive class, *You won't learn anything while you listen to me!* Dialects are not static. As groups become socially or geographically separated, dialects change. Lowe and Graham (1998) suggest that some traditional dialects may even be dying out because of increased geographical mobility, education and the influence of the media.

Accent, for example, a Brummie (Birmingham) accent or a Scottish accent, refers to the regional features of the way we speak English. It is also used to describe speaking a second language with the intonation of the first language, for example *schoolboy French*, a label sometimes given to the way novice learners of the French language, speak it with an English accent.

How you doin' me duck?

I am exceedingly well thank you.

There is no good reason why one accent should be seen as better than another, yet it is human nature to make judgements about the way others speak. Because our language is an indicator of our social group some accents are valued more highly than others. Standard English is sometimes viewed as the gold standard. Nevertheless, with so many regional programmes, such as *Coronation Street*, on TV, the divisions are becoming increasingly blurred.

We also make judgements about the language used in different workplace contexts. Because some occupations are valued more highly than others, the working language for those occupations is also valued highly, although there is no good reason why it should be. The following story (Fromkin et al, 2003, p475) illustrates this point. During cross-examination at a trial, a seaman witness was chastised by the attorney because he didn't understand the meaning of the word *plaintiff*. The attorney had asked him why he had come to the court not knowing its meaning. Later in the trial the seaman used the phrase *abaft the binnacle* to describe where he was standing at the time of the incident. When this was met by a questioning glare from the attorney, the seaman asked him why he had come to court not knowing the meaning of the words *abaft the binnacle*.

Varieties of English

Language isn't static; its changes reflect the social and economic changes in society. For example words such as *typing* and *air hostess* are now rarely used; they have gone out of fashion or are no longer relevant or appropriate. At the same time, new words and phrases such as *networking* and *credit crunch* are taken up, initially, by a few and then by the masses. With each generation, there is the desire to embrace new words. You may remember some popular words from previous generations, for example, *fruity, fab*, which now sound out of place. Change is also reflected in acceptable contemporary grammar, for example the increasingly frequent use of a plural verb with a singular collective noun, for example, *the family are claiming compensation* rather than the strictly correct *the family is claiming compensation*.

There is an extraordinarily wide range of variation in contemporary English. To illustrate this let's look at some of these varieties.

Standard English

The term Standard English is usually used to describe the language of prestigious or powerful people such as political leaders. It is sometimes referred to as *The Queen's English* or *Received Pronunciation (RP)*, and has the formal structure of written English. Nor is there just one Standard English but many: for example, Standard American English, Standard Australian English, Standard Caribbean English, and so on.

Global English

Once English spread to other parts of the world it changed and developed to form new similar, but distinct, varieties and there are now in the region of a billion people worldwide who understand it.

> *English is without a doubt a global language. However, these phenomenal numbers of people do not speak an identical, invariant, unchanging language. Every language is a composite of many different dialects and the further it spreads, the more this is true.*
>
> (Lowe and Graham, 1998, p146)

The reasons for the spread of English are connected to Britain's history of trade and imperialism. It is maintained through its status as the *lingua franca*, the language of choice, for international social and commercial communication. The media is also a powerful instrument of maintenance, in particular, the accessibility of English speaking radio, TV and cinema. In addition, as Mackey (1987) points out, there is often an economic necessity for people to learn English in order to find work.

Estuary English

Lowe and Graham (1998) refer to the emergence of a new regional dialect called Estuary English, a compromise between Standard English and Cockney. They give the example of Joanna Lumley's (Standard English) accent crossed with Frank Bruno's (Cockney) accent producing the Estuary English of Ben Elton. It originated after the Second World War when many of the slums in the east end of London were demolished and the inhabitants moved out into new housing in surrounding counties. Estuary English has spread quickly due to increased commuting, the influence of the media and the gradual loss of prestige associated with Standard English.

Black English Vernacular (BEV)

Spoken mainly in American inner-city ghettos, BEV is spoken by Americans of African descent and is seen as an independent dialect of English. Its features include double negation, for example, *He don't like nothing*, and the deletion of the verb *to be*, for example, *He OK* and *It mine* in place of *He is OK* and *It is mine*. Fromkin et al suggest that the emergence of BEV is due partly to the historical discrimination that created the isolated social environment for it to develop and, more recently, because many black people want to be positively identified with their own dialect.

Trucker talk

David Crystal (2002) describes a variety of contemporary English, used by American truckers as a jargon for communicating routine messages, popularised in the film *Convoy.* Here are some examples.

anklebiters	children	**bear den**	police station
doughnuts	tyres	**eyeballs**	headlights
grandma lane	slow lane	**lettuce**	paper money
mobile mattress	car and caravan	**motion lotion**	fuel

The language of technology

ICT has been responsible for a huge number of new words, such as *chatrooms* and *blogs*. Online communication also requires fast, easy ways to get messages across so this has led to the emergence of acronyms such as PONA (Person Of No Account) and MUDs (Multi-User Dimensions). Another method for passing messages quickly is by using Smilies. Here are a few examples.

Surprised	:o	Crying	:'(
Don't tell anyone	:-#	Sad	:-(
Confused	:-S	I don't know	:^)

Multilingualism and bilingualism

We say that someone is multilingual when they are able to use several languages with equal fluency. Bilingualism, the most common form, is when someone is able to use two languages fluently.

> *Speaking two or more languages is the natural way of life for three-quarters of the human race.*
>
> (Crystal, 2005, p409)

Fromkin et al (2003) offer us some insight into how someone becomes bilingual. Quoting research by Johnson and Newport, they suggest that age is a critical factor. Children who acquire a second language before the age of nine generally become native speakers. Children are uniformly successful in achieving bilingualism across the spectrum of language and nationality. Mackey (1987, p305) gives an account of a six-year-old Spanish girl, placed in a completely French environment, who appeared to lose her Spanish in 93 days and could speak French as well as any French child within a year. For every year above the age of nine there appears to be a decline in the degree of fluency.

In the process of acquiring two languages children develop a separate grammar structure and discrete vocabulary for each language. They also appear to use the two languages in different circumstances, acquiring the appropriate vocabulary for each. For example, a child may learn certain words relevant to home, such as *bath* and *teddy*, in one language and other words relevant to school, such as *classroom* and *playground*, in the other.

Fromkin et al suggest that, unless immensely talented, adults are unable to learn another language without considerable effort. And even then they would not normally be as fluent as a native speaker. Nor, unlike younger children, are they uniformly successful; people vary considerably in their language achievement depending on factors such as their age, motivation and natural talent.

The process of learning a second language as an adult is also different from the one experienced by bilingual children. The learning process passes through a series of intermediate stages; at each stage an appropriate or inter-language grammar is used. One example of the use of inter-language grammar is word order. For example, rather than saying *I have given the book to her*, a German person learning to speak English might say *I have to her the book given* because that phrasing replicates the normal German word order. This is an example of the influence of first language on second language learning in that we unconsciously transfer first language rules and conventions, such as accent and grammar, to the second language. In the above example of the use of inter-language, the native German speaker has transferred the grammar rules relating to word order from their own language to the second language.

> *He that understands grammar in one language understands it in another as far as the essential properties of grammar are concerned. The fact that he can't speak, nor comprehend, another language is due to the diversity of words and their various forms, but these are the accidental properties of grammar.*
>
> (Roger Bacon, 1214–94)

REFLECTIVE TASK

Consider what difficulties you have experienced in learning another language. To what extent do you feel that age, knowledge of grammar and previous language learning have affected your success at learning this language?

Supporting ESOL learners

The importance and relevance of supporting ESOL learners has been highlighted by Christine Gilbert, Ofsted's chief inspector, in a report on training for ESOL learners.

> *Good English-speaking skills open up a world of opportunities and benefits to learners, such as developing skills for the workplace and integrating further with*

the community. We must equip learners with the very best English skills to help them have the confidence to make a positive contribution to the community.

(*The Independent*, 3 October, 2008)

The Adult ESOL Core Curriculum (DfES, 2001) estimates that around a million adults in England have a first language other than English. This figure includes settled communities, refugees, some of whom may be asylum seekers, migrant workers and partners and spouses.

What sort of experience do these learners have and what can we do to support them? To explore some of the answers we are going to return to Hai Ling who you met in earlier chapters. Here she is talking about her experiences of work and learning since she came to England.

CASE STUDY – HAI LING

I was very keen to come to England as my husband is English and we think we will both have better job prospects here. My English is good; I was an English teacher in Shanghai for over ten years. I speak Mandarin, Shanghai dialect and some Spanish. My experience of learning since I have been here has been studying for the citizenship test, undertaking a marketing course and taking Spanish lessons. I now wish to develop my ICT skills.

I work in the administration department of a university. It has been a good experience for me because it has given me the opportunity to really develop my English. My employers funded a marketing course which I have found very interesting. At first I was surprised because students here are expected to contribute and take part in discussions. Also the students are very happy to challenge the teacher. This would rarely happen in China; students there sit in rows and listen to the teacher. Politeness is extremely important to us.

Studying for the citizenship test was interesting also. Initially, I didn't think I would learn very much but I have found it has been very useful. For example, I now know how to rent an apartment or make an offer on a property. This is all new to me.

PRACTICAL TASK PRACTICAL TASK **PRACTICAL TASK** PRACTICAL TASK **PRACTICAL TASK**

What can you draw from Hai Ling's comments that would give you a greater understanding of learners from different cultures?

You may have identified some of the following points.

- Hai Ling has received a good education with a sound understanding of English grammar. She has been educated in a society that values learning. and is very motivated to learn. She is also a speaker of more than one language and is able to use her knowledge to support her learning. This shows us that we need to be aware that ESOL learners will have very diverse backgrounds; some may have limited education, others, like Hai Ling, will be highly educated professionals.
- Hai Ling has come to England with her husband and was very keen to make that transition as it has opened up career possibilities. Not all learners will be as happy to

be here and may have had little choice about leaving their own country. Some may have had to flee their country because of oppression or natural disaster.

- In the two years since she has been in England Hai Ling has settled into a job, taken the citizenship test, undertaken a marketing course, begun to improve her Spanish and plans to improve her ICT skills. She has achieved certain of her goals and knows what she needs to do next. Learners will have many different goals and needs in a variety of educational and work-based contexts.

- Hai Ling's education in China was very different to her experiences here. It was more disciplined and regimented, with considerable emphasis on politeness. This shows us that learners from other societies may have very different culturally determined attitudes to learning.

We'll return again to Hai Ling. This time she is talking about speaking, reading and writing English.

CASE STUDY – HAI LING

In China it is not part of our culture to talk to strangers, and especially foreigners, so it can be difficult for Chinese people here to speak in class. There is also the psychological barrier connected to our history; some Chinese people have feelings of inferiority which make it difficult for them to relax. It can sometimes look as though a Chinese person doesn't know the answer when in fact they know very well.

Even though my English is good I still need to read English fairly slowly. It isn't that I don't understand the vocabulary; it's just the difference in the way the two languages are structured. Chinese sentences have far more pauses. We have a different system of punctuation as well. Although we now use western punctuation marks, traditionally we use words; for example, we use the word ma *which means a question, in place of a question mark.*

Learning English can be quite difficult for Chinese people. It is not so much because we have a different alphabet but more because English and Chinese are written in a different style. Chinese is not logical but relies much more on metaphor and poetic allusion. English vocabulary also poses a problem because there is no common root base. Since I began learning Spanish I realise how easy it is for Europeans to learn other European languages because so many words have a similar base. People here also have a shared history which must make any learning that much easier. In one of my classes the teacher was getting us to work in pairs talking about Anthony and Cleopatra. I didn't even know who they were.

I am getting quite good now at understanding English idiom because I have been working hard at it but I still get confused when friends tell jokes. Everyone else is laughing their heads off (idiom!) and I'm sitting there with a straight face (more idiom!).

PRACTICAL TASK PRACTICAL TASK PRACTICAL TASK PRACTICAL TASK PRACTICAL TASK

Imagine Hai Ling is one of your learners. What can you learn from her comments that could help you in supporting her as a learner?

You may have thought of some of the following.

- You would need to give her plenty of time to read handouts, etc. People who are from countries whose language is very different from English might need more time than perhaps someone from another European country even if their English appears to be excellent. The amount of concentration required means they are likely to tire and lose concentration towards the end of a session so their performance may deteriorate later in the day.
- You will need to give her opportunities to talk in a small group and provide gentle encouragement until she is confident to contribute to class discussions. You need to be sensitive to the fact that people from other cultures may have different communication rules and conventions. If they have been led to believe that teachers are always correct and should never be contradicted they are likely to be reluctant to ask questions or engage in discussion. Similarly, learners from a culture that lays stress on the importance of 'face' may be reluctant to volunteer information through fear of appearing wrong in front of their colleagues. A question like *Do you understand*? is likely to be answered in the affirmative even if the learner doesn't have any idea about the meaning of the topic.
- You would need to be very careful when using idiom, jargon and making jokes. You would also need to avoid, or explain, culturally specific material remembering that some learners may have little shared history.

There is one more point we can learn from Hai Ling. She recognises how useful her work experience has been for developing her English speaking and writing skills.

> *The socio-cultural paradigm stresses the role of contextual, social factors in literacy acquisition and usage. Findings from this research suggest that people acquire language and literacy by being informally socialised into the practices and values of context in which they are immersed.*
>
> (Auerbach, 2006, p56)

This important point has been emphasised in the companion guide, which points out that one of the most effective ways to learn another language is to do it in any other way than sitting in a classroom and learning vocabulary and grammar. It goes on to say that *many very proficient second language speakers have never attended any formal classes, rather they have acquired their second language through work and everyday life* (LLUK, November 2007, p38).

We see here the importance of context in language learning. We are already working to develop literacy and language skills within the context of subject specialisms. Clearly, an integrated approach appears to be just as appropriate for ESOL learners provided we are sensitive to the specific barriers that are part and parcel of learning in an unfamiliar country using a second, third or even fourth language.

Supporting all learners

We said earlier that your learners may well demonstrate a wide variety of English dialect and accent and that this diversity needs to be acknowledged and valued while extending learners' language and literacy skills. The companion guide gives a number of examples of good practice for communicating with ESOL learners. However, the guide also emphasises their application to communicating with all learners. A number of these examples have already been covered in the discussion of Hai Ling's experience, but you will find them, plus the following suggestions, especially helpful when communicating with learners with a variety of English backgrounds.

- Set the scene at the beginning of a session, where necessary, pre-teaching key words, terms and phrases and using visual and verbal cues, to indicate key points.
- Repeat key ideas and learning points and highlight them on the board.
- Keep explanations short, speak clearly and back up with handouts.
- Give learners time to answer questions, check understanding and avoid questions that require a yes or no answer.

These points are covered in greater detail in Chapters 7–11.

A SUMMARY OF KEY POINTS

> There are in the region of a billion people worldwide who understand English.

> Generally, people become bilingual through the acquisition of two languages as young children.

> There are numerous varieties of English; one variety isn't necessarily superior or inferior to another.

> We each have our own idiolect or personal way of speaking.

> Accent and dialect reflect our attachment to social and/or geographical groups.

> In supporting learners we need to be sensitive to the cultural and linguistic differences that can affect learning.

> Developing language and literacy skills within context is important for all learners.

Branching options

The following tasks are designed to help you consolidate and develop your understanding of multilingualism and language diversity.

Reflection

How would you describe your idiolect? Has it changed during the course of your life, and if so in what ways? Consider and note the reasons for this.

Analysis

Dakshi is attending one of your part-time classes. He is now 26 and was born in Bihar. He went to school in India and is bilingual in Hindi and Urdu. Eight years ago he arrived in England with his parents, and they set up business by opening an Indian restaurant in Gateshead. He speaks English quite well with a pronounced Geordie accent, but his written English is poor.

What strategies could you use to help Dakshi develop his English language skills while he is attending your classes?

Research

Research the background of any learners in your classes who have a first language other than English. What barriers to learning are these learners likely to experience?

REFERENCES AND FURTHER READING REFERENCES AND FURTHER READING

Auerbach, E (2006) Aligning socio-cultural and critical approaches to multilingual literacy research. In Tett, L et al (eds) *Adult literacy, numeracy and language: policy, practice and research.* Maidenhead: Open University Press.

Crystal, D (2002) *The English language.* London: Penguin.

Crystal, D (2005) *How language works*. London: Penguin.

DfES (2001) *Adult ESOL Core Curriculum* London: DfES.

Fromkin, V, Rodman, R and Hyams, N (2003) *An introduction to language.* Boston, MA: Thomson Heinle.

LLUK (November 2007) *Inclusive learning approaches for literacy, language, numeracy and ICT.* London: LLUK (the companion guide).

Lowe, M and Graham, B (1998) *English language for beginners.* London: Writers and Readers.

Mackey, W (1987) The description of bilingualism. In Mayor, B and Pugh, AK (eds) *Language, communication and education.* Beckenham: Croom Helm.

Walters, J (2008) *That's another story*. London: Weidenfeld & Nicolson.

7
Speaking and listening

This chapter will help you to:

* explore the theory of speaking and listening;
* investigate how you can use this understanding to develop your own skills and those of your learners.

Links to minimum core elements:

A 2.1   Making appropriate choices in oral communication episodes.
A 2.2   Having a knowledge of fluency, accuracy and competence for ESOL learners.
A 2.3   Using spoken English effectively.
A 2.4   Listening effectively.
B 1   Expressing yourself clearly, using communication techniques to help convey meaning and to enhance the delivery and accessibility of the message.
B 2   Showing the ability to use language, style and tone in ways that suit the intended audience.
B 3   Using appropriate techniques to reinforce oral communication, check how well the information is received and support the understanding of those listening.
B 5   Listening attentively and responding sensitively to contributions made by others.

Links to LLUK Professional Standards for QTLS:
AS4, AS7, AK5.1, BK2.2, BP2.2, BK3.1, BK3.2, BK3.3, BK3.4, BP3.1, BP3.2, BP3.3, BP3.4, CK3.4, CP3.4.

Links to LLUK mandatory units of assessment:
Planning and enabling learning (CTLLS and DTLLS):

* **understand how to use a range of communication skills and methods to communicate effectively with learners and relevant parties in own organisation;**
* **understand and demonstrate knowledge of the minimum core in own practice.**

Enabling learning and assessment (DTLLS):

* **understand and demonstrate how to give effective feedback to promote learner progress and achievement;**
* **understand and demonstrate knowledge of the minimum core in own practice.**

Theories and principles for planning and enabling learning (DTLLS):

* **understand and demonstrate knowledge of the minimum core in own practice.**

Introduction

We don't really know when human beings first acquired language but we do know that, once acquired, it became essential, for co-operation, and in order to negotiate our highly complex environment. As human society has developed and diversified our pool of language has increased. Even Shakespeare, who has been credited with the first recorded use of over 2,000 words and phrases, didn't have the depth and variety of language we now have at our disposal (Bryson, 2007).

We are constantly involved in speaking and listening, so much so that it would be difficult to imagine life without it. We saw in Chapter 3 that most of us learn to speak and understand language very early in our lives, so early, we probably have little or no recollection of doing so. It is automatic; we don't think too much about how we do it.

This chapter is all about being aware of how we speak and listen and importantly, being aware of how we speak and listen to learners. It is almost impossible to think of teaching without speaking and listening. Even with modern communication technology it is still very much at the heart of our interaction with our learners. You could say that a teacher with good speaking and listening skills is very likely to be a good teacher.

In this chapter we will explore the nature and theory of speaking and listening and investigate how you can use this knowledge to develop your speaking and listening skills. We will then look at how you can apply these skills in your interaction with learners and help them develop their own speaking and listening skills.

The nature and theory of speaking and listening

We can begin by saying that speaking and listening is an interaction between two or more people. (This isn't strictly true of course – you can have some very good conversations with yourself – but we will assume for our purposes that it is.) Clearly, you need people: one to speak and at least one to listen.

So, what happens when someone speaks and someone else listens? It appears at first glance to be very straightforward; words are spoken by one person and listened to by another. But a closer look reveals a third element, non-verbal communication. This is the topic of the next chapter, so we just need to note here that non-verbal communication supports and enhances spoken language.

A closer look at speaking and listening also reveals a number of other important aspects:

- communication is a process;
- speaking and listening are purpose-led;
- there are significant differences between speaking and writing;
- speaking and listening do not take place in a vacuum but within a context;
- we interpret what we hear in a way that makes sense to us;
- there are a number of potential barriers that can disrupt the communication process.

An awareness of these aspects will assist us in developing our speaking and listening skills. Let's look at each in turn.

The communication process

The communication process is often expressed in the form of a diagrammatical model. The best-known model, and one that appears frequently in communication books, is by Shannon and Weaver represented here in Figure 7.1. Although limited in its scope, the model provides us with a reasonable starting point.

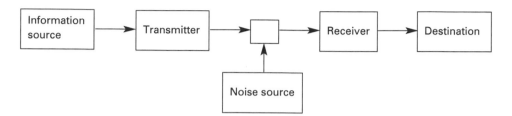

Figure 7.1 Shannon and Weaver's model of communication (Fiske, 1990)

In the context of speaking and listening, the information source in the model is the thought or intended meaning in the speaker's mind and the transmitter is the speaker's voice. Similarly, the receiver is the listener's ear and the destination is the listener's understanding of the message. Noise refers to any interference that distorts the message.

Although it might appear be a one-way system, i.e. words passing from A to B, and is depicted this way in Shannon and Weaver's model, in reality it is a dual system in as much as the listener is also active. The listener will use verbal signals such as *Yes*, or *I agree,* to encourage the speaker to continue, and words like *Sorry? eh?* or *um,* to signal to the speaker to stop or repeat something. In fact, messages are passed continuously between speaker and listener and each is likely to adjust and modify what they say in response to the other. Each speaker will know when to speak and will take turns in the conversation. Stenstrom (1996) refers to a general atmosphere of co-operation and harmony that is present in interpersonal communication.

Speaking and listening are purpose-led

PRACTICAL TASK PRACTICAL TASK PRACTICAL TASK PRACTICAL TASK PRACTICAL TASK

Think for a few minutes about a conversation you had earlier today, or yesterday if it is more practical. It doesn't matter whether it was a long conversation or just a couple of words. What purpose do you think it served? Note your response and compare with the comments below.

Stevens (1975) identifies a number of purposes of spoken language. Here are some of the most common.

You want to obtain something
Language has a number of practical purposes. You might have ordered a coffee in a cafe this morning. Someone might have asked you to pass over the free newspaper.

You need information, an answer, or a solution to a problem

This is another practical reason we use language. When something needs sorting out one way is to ask someone. Perhaps you asked some learners whether they could hear your voice clearly, or a colleague asked you if you knew what was wrong with the photocopier.

You enjoy other people's company

Perhaps you had a chance to chat with a friend. Most of us use language for the pleasure of it. We enjoy being with others and language offers us an opportunity to experience and reinforce relationships.

This social aspect of language is an important one. Consider what happens when you meet someone in the street, a neighbour perhaps, or an acquaintance. You will probably say something along the lines of, *Hi, how are you?* And they will reply, *Fine, how are you?* Greetings follow the established rules or conventions of conversation and we all know what to expect. You may indeed be interested in how your neighbour or acquaintance is feeling but this verbal interaction is doing far more than enquiring after each other's health. It is cementing the relationships we have with others and is sometimes referred to as social glue. Zoologist Desmond Morris (1986) calls it grooming talk because primates greet each other with mutual grooming as a means of promoting group cohesion.

You want to inform or influence someone

You may have told a group of learners about a forthcoming assessment. You may have asked them to listen carefully because you had something important to say. Sometimes we want to influence the way other people see us. Most of us have tried to make a good impression at an interview or a party.

You were expressing your feelings

We use language to express feelings such as anger, pleasure, irritation, love, etc. For example, you may tell your learners that you are really pleased with their hard work.

Differences between speaking and writing

There are significant differences between speaking and writing.

- We speak using words and phrases and, apart from formal occasions such as giving a presentation, we tend to speak off the cuff, without too much thought or planning. Written English is usually in sentence form and tends to be planned.
- Spoken English has an informal structure. Our conversation may include colloquial language and slang, for example, *he nicked my pen*, and *she eats a lot of junk food*. Idiom, i.e., phrases where the combined meaning of the words is different from their individual meaning, also plays a greater role in speaking. Some examples of idiom are *down in the dumps* and *fly off the handle*.
- Spoken English is supported by non-verbal communication. We use a range of voice changes, facial expressions and gestures for emphasis and to convey meaning. For example, we use a rising tone to indicate a question. Written English uses textual features, such as punctuation and language style for emphasis and to convey meaning. For example, we use inverted commas to indicate direct speech.

REFLECTIVE TASK

Try reading these phrases out loud and then repeat each as a question. Note how your voice changes to convey the meaning.

He understands the question.
We'll go this way.

Speaking and listening take place within a context

When we talk about context in relation to speaking and listening, we are referring to the relationship, shared experience, attitudes and expectations of those involved, as well as the cultural and physical setting.

Think for a moment about how we use technical language and jargon within context. It is understood only by those in the know. The education arena is no exception. We use words and phrases, such as *learning outcomes* and *minimum core*, which may have little meaning for others. When we use educational jargon its meaning is understood only because it is expressed in context, i.e., within the education arena, between those with a shared experience.

PRACTICAL TASK PRACTICAL TASK PRACTICAL TASK PRACTICAL TASK PRACTICAL TASK PRACTICAL TASK

Cast your mind back to the last time you walked into a classroom and greeted a group of learners. Try to recall the way you greeted them. Now imagine going into a school classroom and greeting a group of eight-year-old learners. How would you alter your greeting? Compare your response with the comments below.

Here are some of the ways your greeting might change.

- You might speak more slowly to make sure the learners hear and understand you. (Or you might speak more quickly because you are nervous.)
- You smile more because they are children.
- You change the style of your greeting, i.e. use vocabulary more appropriate for children.

This task reveals the relationship between context and the communication process, and we are usually skilled at ensuring the process is appropriate to the context. It's appropriate for us to speak using informal colloquial language and slang when relaxing in the pub with friends but less so in a teaching context.

The concept of appropriacy in a teaching context is an important one. We need to look at it carefully and we will begin by looking at what we can learn from one teacher's experience of inappropriate language.

SCENARIO STUDY – FRANKLIN – A PROBLEM OF LANGUAGE

Franklin is a lecturer in the Management Studies Department of his local college with a specialism in Health and Safety. He is studying for a QTLS qualification and is writing in his personal journal after a very uncomfortable classroom experience. He has been delivering an NCFE Occupational Health and Safety course in the training centre of a large engineering firm and his learners are all supervisors employed by the firm.

I'm writing this up straight away while it's still going round in my head. I'm so angry with myself. I just let it happen. Everything seemed to be going OK. They seemed to be a nice group of guys. They were pretty relaxed. I suppose it was because they all knew each other and were on home ground. It was when I asked them to work in small groups to talk about a past experience of a dangerous occurrence and report back on what they had learned, that things began to go wrong. Phil started it. He was talking about some machine operatives and he was saying personal things about them. It made me feel uncomfortable but everyone else seemed OK and then Vince did the same, he started saying things about a colleague. They must be used to it. I don't think they even noticed. I felt pretty bad though because I'd done nothing to stop it. To be honest I felt out of my depth, but I also felt there was something wrong with me, that I was the odd one out and I still can't believe that I was actually going to join in. If Vince hadn't then started using some pretty offensive swear words I'm not sure what would have happened. I made a feeble effort to say that swearing wasn't appropriate but I know it didn't come over very well and I've never been more relieved to reach the end of a session.

PRACTICAL TASK PRACTICAL TASK PRACTICAL TASK PRACTICAL TASK PRACTICAL TASK

Was the language used by Phil and Vince appropriate? Was Franklin right to intervene when he did? Write down you answers and compare them with the notes that follow.

What can we say about Franklin's experience? Clearly, the language in this classroom was inappropriate. It's not difficult though to see how Franklin was almost drawn in against his better judgement. He felt isolated and began to wonder whether he was being unreasonable in his expectations. We can now say that his expectations were not unreasonable. Franklin just didn't have the confidence to stop the discussion immediately things began to go wrong and tell the learners very clearly that their language wasn't appropriate.

Hindsight is indeed wonderful, but when we are engaged in building a good rapport with learners it is all too easy to adapt our language style to theirs. But emulating our learners will not help them to develop their speaking and listening skills. One of the best strategies we have at our disposal is our own example. If we provide our learners with a model that clearly and unequivocally demonstrates good practice they will take notice. If we communicate with them in an appropriate and professional manner they will learn to do the same.

We interpret what we hear in a way that makes sense to us

We saw from Shannon and Weaver's communication model (Figure 7.1) that receiving the signal is not the end of the story; the signal has to reach its destination. For us, that destination is our personal understanding of what we hear. Words have a meaningful or semantic interpretation and we are constantly trying to interpret and understand what we hear in a way that makes sense to us. Have you ever been in a situation where something doesn't make sense? Perhaps you have looked at one of those peculiar drawings by Escher which have steps leading nowhere or lines that magically turn into spaces. You stare at the drawing trying to make sense of what you see and when you can't, you feel uncomfortable and disorientated. Some of the tools we have at our disposal to give meaning to what we hear are context, prior knowledge and experience.

There are many stories describing how children seek to give meaning to words that appear meaningless to them. One of my favourites is the child who made sense of the hymn *Gladly the cross I'd bear* by interpreting it as a reference to a bear called Gladly who was cross-eyed. (Stevens, 1975).

Words mean something, of course, but the meaning of any particular word is arbitrary. The word *cat* only means a four-legged animal that meows because we have agreed that it should. A four-legged animal that meows is *Katze* in German and *gatto* in Italian. (Onomatopoeic words such as *buzz, whoosh,* etc are the exception.) The arbitrary nature of word meaning leaves room for manoeuvre and word meaning can and does change. Take the word *villain.* At one time it referred to a peasant or a farmer, now it means a criminal.

We said earlier that we use context, prior knowledge and experience to enable us to make sense of the spoken word. But we are all individuals; each of us has unique knowledge and experience. It follows then that the same word could have many meanings; you could say potentially a different meaning for every person. Nor do we always realise that we *do* see the meaning of words differently. It is not difficult to see how this could lead to confusion. Here is a story that illustrates this point.

One day a king called one of his ministers and told him to go and bring all the men of the town that were born blind. When the blind men had been assembled, the king told a servant: Show these men an elephant. *The servant did as he was commanded and he made one blind man touch the head of the elephant, another the ear, another the trunk, a tusk, a foot, the back and the tail, and to each one he said that he was touching the elephant.*

Then the king asked the blind men: Have you studied the elephant? Tell me your conclusions. *The man who had touched the head said:* It is like a pot. *The one who had touched the ear said:* It is like a fan. *And so for the others the trunk became a plough; a tusk, a ploughshare; a foot, a pillar; the back, a granary; and the tail a broom. And each blind man thought that what he had touched was the elephant. Then they began to argue with each other and to quarrel, saying:* An elephant is like this – no, it is not, it is like this. *And so on.*

(Adapted from Mascaro, 1961)

This story illustrates an important point for us as teachers. Our learners need to make sense of what we say to them. Do we make this easy for them by explaining carefully and checking that their understanding is the same as our meaning? *We* know what we mean. Have we made it clear to learners? Just like the blind men, each of our learners will construct their own meaning from our words. It is perhaps especially important to keep this in mind when we are communicating with learners who may have very different life experiences from ourselves, who may be from a different culture or for whom English is not their first language.

Barriers can disrupt the speaking and listening process

Barriers to communication, referred to in Shannon and Weaver's communication model as noise, are many and varied. Obviously, factors such as background noise or a learner's poor hearing could disrupt the process. But there are many other reasons why we don't always hear what is said. We may, for example, be prejudiced against what is being said, either because we are not interested or we don't agree. Sometimes we have difficulty hearing because the speaker has poor communication skills, is nervous, or uses unusual vocabulary, jargon, colloquial language, or unfamiliar idiom or dialect. This can pose a particular problem for people from different cultures and for learners with autistic spectrum disorder.

Let's now look at a trainee teacher's experience to see how barriers can disrupt the speaking and listening process in the classroom.

SCENARIO STUDY – CATHY – DID ANYONE NOT UNDERSTAND THAT?

Cathy is a trainee teacher working towards QTLS. Her specialist subject is childcare and she is just about to begin class with a group of learners working towards a Foundation Award in Caring for Children (Level 1). Cathy has a genuine interest in her young learners and is really keen for them to do well in their studies.

It is a Monday morning in January and when Cathy enters the classroom and greets her learners she asks them if they had a good weekend. She is vaguely conscious that the central heating is very slow in getting started and the room feels chilly, but she is thinking more about how much she needs to tell her learners and how time is short.

OK! she says. *This is what I want to do this morning*.

Cathy then launches into a long description of the most common childhood ailments and how to recognise their symptoms. She speaks fairly quickly because there is a lot to say, and continues with few pauses, producing a constant stream of words, which includes a number of medical terms such as rubella and diagnostic.

As she talks to the learners, she moves around the room, sitting, first on the front of the desk, then behind it, then moving across to the window to see what is making that awful humming noise outside. She isn't aware that the humming noise has been present for most of the session or that she has increased the volume of her voice in response and that she now has the beginnings of a sore throat.

Half an hour later Cathy is happy that she has passed on everything she knows about childhood ailments to her learners, so she stops. *Did you all understand that?* she asks. None of the learners replies so she asks, *Did anyone not understand that?* Again silence. Unaware that most of the learners just want to get up and move around to warm up and that if they respond to her questions this will be delayed, Cathy is pleased that the session has gone so well.

How could Cathy minimise the barriers with her learners?

Instead of launching straight into her topic Cathy should have introduced it carefully, using words and phrases to signal its content. This would have given her learners an opportunity to think about what might be coming. It would have been far better though if she had begun by asking them what they knew about the topic. Alternatively, they could have discussed the topic in small groups. Some of her learners probably had younger brothers and sisters or babysitting jobs and would have significant input in a discussion about childhood ailments. Speaking to other learners in this structured way is an opportunity for them to develop their own speaking and listening skills. This strategy might also have helped to solve the problem of the background noise and saved Cathy's voice.

We don't know about the clarity of Cathy's speech but, as she was in a hurry, we can probably assume that her learners did not understand all of her points. If she had taken her time, had spoken clearly and used her voice to emphasise important points she would have minimised the potential for her learners to misunderstand her meaning.

Cathy should have used key words and phrases, such as *next we are going to ...* and. *Any questions before we move on?* to make it clear that she was moving on to the next point. These would have provided an opportunity for her to check understanding.

She should have structured her speech logically, reinforcing important points to allow the learners to predict what might be following and carefully explained the meaning of the medical words and phrases to make sure that the learners understood. She could have put key information on the board. Visual aids might also have been useful.

Cathy is vaguely aware when she walks in that the room is chilly, but does nothing about it. She has been moving around so is unlikely to be feeling as cold as the learners who have been sitting still. Frozen learners are unlikely to listen attentively.

Even supposing that the learners were prepared to put aside how cold they were feeling and talk to Cathy, her use of closed questions, that required only a yes or no answer, to check understanding gave them little incentive to speak. Nor would an affirmative answer to the question have helped. Her only real way of knowing that they understood would have been to ask open-ended questions, such as *What can you say about...?* and, *What would you do if...?*

Poor Cathy, for thinking everything was fine when it clearly wasn't, and poor, poor learners for sitting still in a cold classroom, although they do appear to be unusually reticent.

Before we leave Cathy, do you recall that she automatically raised her voice in response to the humming noise outside? The question of how loud to speak is an interesting one. We certainly need to speak loudly enough to be heard but it is easy to get into the habit of speaking too loudly. When I was a trainee teacher I was lucky enough to observe a very experienced teacher. I was immediately struck by how quietly he spoke to the learners and by the fact that they all appeared to be able to hear easily. Seated right at the back of the classroom, I too, could hear him clearly. At the end of the session I asked him why he spoke so quietly. *That's easy,* he said, *the quieter I speak the more they practise their listening skills.* At the next session I watched him and realised that, although he spoke quietly, he always looked at the learners, spoke slowly and clearly and emphasised every syllable. His method may not suit every teacher but there is much we can learn from it. If we always look at learners when we speak to them and speak clearly, sounding all the syllables, it can be more effective than raising our voices.

PRACTICAL TASK PRACTICAL TASK PRACTICAL TASK PRACTICAL TASK PRACTICAL TASK

Think about a recent teaching situation. What barriers to communication can you identify? What could you do to minimise them? Note this in your journal.

Developing your speaking and listening skills with learners

We have seen that speaking and listening are part of a complex process that can easily be disrupted. Our task as teachers is to make this process as smooth as possible and to minimise potential barriers so that our learners understand what we mean and we understand what they mean. In short, we need to be good communicators. When this process works smoothly our learners will recognise and use it as a template for developing their own speaking and listening skills.

REFLECTIVE TASK

How would you describe someone who is a good communicator?

You might think that a good communicator is someone who can give a slick presentation or who is comfortable speaking to a large audience, but this isn't necessarily the case. In fact, a good communicator is much more likely to be someone who is an effective listener and who asks the right questions (Wallace, 2007). These are important skills for us as teachers and worth looking at in detail.

Effective listening

To listen effectively your listening needs to be active. This means taking care to pay close attention to what someone is saying. You need also to signal your close attention by using words and phrases such as *I see* and *Go on.* This will show the speaker that you are listening and will encourage them to continue.

Paraphrasing and summarising someone's words are useful techniques for developing effective listening skills. Paraphrasing means conveying the meaning of something using different words. Summarising means giving a brief account of what you hear. They also show the speaker that you have listened, because it's impossible to paraphrase or summarise accurately unless you do listen carefully. Paraphrasing and summarising require more concentration than you would think.

Effective questioning

We want to draw learners in, to make them think and to encourage them to express their ideas and opinions. Asking the right questions can achieve this.

Closed questions

We saw how Cathy checked her learners' understanding of childhood ailments by asking two questions: *Did you all understand that?* and *Did anyone not understand that?* These are both examples of closed questions. Closed questions have a limited range of short answers and are best reserved for checking specific facts, for example, *What is the capital of Norway?*

Open questions

Open questions such as *What do you know about ...?* and *what would you do if ...?* are more effective for involving learners in a topic. They stimulate thought processes and encourage learners to engage in discussion.

Supporting learners

Clearly, we want to encourage and support our learners in developing their own speaking and listening skills, and the best way to achieve this is by providing them with an example that is clear and consistent.

When we use our speaking and listening skills effectively in the classroom our learners will learn from us. When we give them opportunities to speak and listen they will gain confidence. When we give them positive but honest feedback to show that we respect their opinion and value what they have to say, they will learn to do the same with those around them. When we set the standard of professional and appropriate communication our learners will develop their speaking and listening skills according to the model we provide.

Here are some general points to bear in mind for supporting learners.

Speaking

- Always use appropriate language and expect the same from learners.
- Speak clearly, at a pace and volume which are easy for learners to hear.
- Use the tone and pace of your voice to emphasise important points and to make your topic interesting.
- Speak in a logical sequence, structuring your speech with key words to reinforce important points and markers to indicate to learners that you are moving on to the next point.

- Paraphrase important or complex points as you speak to ensure that learners interpret your words in the correct way.
- Always explain when you use technical words and check that all of your learners understand what they mean.
- Back up important points on the board and with handouts.
- Don't attempt to speak against background noise. Instead, be flexible and use other ways to get points across.
- Make sure that learners are physically comfortable, that everyone can see and hear and the room is not too hot or cold. Break up sessions so that learners do not become physically uncomfortable or tired.
- Where individual learners experience difficulties that could interfere with their understanding, make sure they receive appropriate help.
- Try to avoid, where possible, using culturally specific language, jargon or idiom as learners from other cultures may not understand and could feel isolated.

Listening

- Listen actively, paying careful attention to what learners have to say.
- Be open. Don't have preconceptions or assume that something might not be relevant.
- Paraphrase or summarise learners' contributions to show that you have listened and understood and back up important points on the board.
- If possible, don't interrupt when a learner is speaking.
- Give appropriate verbal and non-verbal listening signals (see next chapter).

Asking questions

- Ask open questions to draw learners into the topic.
- Give learners time to answer. They will need to think about what is involved and consider what they are going to say. If they struggle to find an answer resist the temptation to supply the answer yourself.
- Give positive, but honest feedback. Words and phrases like *good start* and *can you say more about*...? will give them confidence and encourage them to continue.
- Try, as far as possible, to avoid interrupting a learner who is speaking.

A SUMMARY OF KEY POINTS

> Speaking and listening is an interaction between two or more people.

> We speak and listen for a purpose.

> There are significant differences between spoken and written English.

> Speaking and listening are part of the process of interpersonal communication.

> Speaking and listening take place within a context.

> We interpret what we hear in a way that has meaning for us.

> Barriers can disrupt the speaking and listening process.

> Speaking skills include using appropriate language, speaking clearly and logically, explaining technical words, checking understanding and backing up important points.

> Active listening includes appropriate verbal and non-verbal feedback, paraphrasing and summarising where appropriate.

> Questioning skills include using open and closed questions appropriately and giving learners time to answer.

Branching options

The following tasks are designed to help you consolidate and develop your understanding of speaking and listening.

Reflection

In this chapter we have emphasised that our learners need to make sense of what we say to them. Consider and list the ways that we can ensure this happens and note which of these strategies work for you in your next lessons.

Analysis

Make an audio recording of a segment of one of your lessons in which you are giving information or an explanation, probably lasting around ten minutes. When you play back this segment, analyse your presentation and note in your journal those areas where you feel your speaking techniques could be developed further.

Research

Is Shannon and Weaver's communication model (Figure 7.1) appropriate to explain the speaking and listening activities that characterise your own teaching? Does this model have limitations, and are there more relevant models that provide a theoretical justification for your approach to speaking and listening in your teaching? Record your findings in your journal.

REFERENCES AND FURTHER READING REFERENCES AND FURTHER READING

Bryson, B (2007) *Shakespeare*. London: HarperCollins.

Fiske, J (1990) *Introduction to communication studies*. London: Routledge.

Gamble, T and Gamble, M (1996*) Communication works.* New York: McGraw–Hill.

Mascaro, J (1961) *Lamps of fire from the scriptures and wisdom of the world*. London: Methuen.

Maybin, J and Mercer, N (1996) *Using English*. London: Routledge.

Morris, D (1986) *The naked ape.* London: Jonathan Cape.

Stenstrom, A (1996) *An introduction to spoken interaction*. Harlow: Longman.

Stevens, R (1975) Unit 7: Interpersonal communication, in Open University (ed) *Communication*. Buckingham: Open University Press.

Wallace, S (2007) *Teaching, tutoring and training in the lifelong learning sector*. Exeter: Learning Matters.

8
Non-verbal communication

This chapter will help you to:

- understand the importance of non-verbal communication (NVC);
- consider why we use NVC;
- explore how you can use NVC effectively with learners.

Links to minimum core elements:

A 2.4   Listening effectively.

B 1   Expressing yourself clearly, using communication techniques to help convey meaning and to enhance the delivery and accessibility of the message.

B 3   Using appropriate techniques to reinforce oral communication, check how well the information is received and support the understanding of those listening.

B 4   Using non-verbal communication to assist in conveying meaning and receiving information and recognising its use by others.

B 5   Listening attentively and responding sensitively to contributions made by others.

Links to LLUK Professional Standards for QTLS:
AS4, AS7, AK5.1, BK2.2, BP2.2, BK3.1, BK3.4, BP3.1, BP3.4, CK3.4, CP3.4.

Links to LLUK mandatory units of assessment:
Planning and enabling learning (CTLLS and DTLLS):

- understand how to use a range of communication skills and methods to communicate effectively with learners and relevant parties in own organisation;
- understand and demonstrate knowledge of the minimum core in own practice.

Enabling learning and assessment (DTLLS):

- understand and demonstrate how to give effective feedback to promote learner progress and achievement;
- understand and demonstrate knowledge of the minimum core in own practice.

Theories and principles for planning and enabling learning (DTLLS):

- understand and demonstrate knowledge of the minimum core in own practice.

Introduction

When you think of non-verbal communication (NVC) you may think of people who wave their hands around when they speak. Hand gestures certainly are one of its features but NVC is much more than this. We communicate non-verbally to support, replace and sometimes even to contradict our words, and the way we do it is ingenious and complex. This is what makes NVC such a fascinating subject to study. Importantly, for us as teachers, an understanding of our non-verbal signals, and those of our learners, is of real value to us in the classroom. So, in this chapter we will explore the concept of NVC and see how you can put this understanding to best practical use in your teaching.

What is NVC?

NVC is a catch-all term that covers the extraordinarily diverse and creative range of ways we communicate with each other over and above the words we speak. The reason for this diversity and creativity is that we are individuals, each of us with our own unique way of doing things.

REFLECTIVE TASK
REFLECTIVE TASK

Think about a person you know pretty well, a family member or a close friend. Is there a particular look they have, a way they perhaps raise an eyebrow or flick their hair, that is instantly recognisable?

Interestingly, despite this diversity, the language of NVC is usually easily understood, and the closer the shared experience of those involved, the more likely this is. As we grow and develop we learn many of the features of NVC from the example and teaching of those closest to us. It isn't surprising then that some of these features are culturally specific. For example, most British people would interpret a fingers crossed sign as a protective gesture to ensure a positive outcome, but in some Mediterranean countries this gesture can signal the end of a friendship (Morris, 2002).

We can divide NVC into three groups. In the first group we can place messages that we convey through the way we use our voice. This is apart from, and in addition to, the words we use and is sometimes referred to as paralanguage. Into the second group we can place messages we convey by the way we use our bodies. This is often referred to as body language and includes facial expression, gesture and posture. Our final group consists of some extras that don't fit under either paralanguage or body language. These are proximity, orientation, appearance and touch. Let's look at these groups one at a time.

Paralanguage

We tend to think about speaking only in terms of the words we use, but our voices speak more than words. Indeed, a greater proportion of our message can be passed through our voice than through our words. If this seems a little difficult to believe, try the following three-part task. You can do it on your own but it is probably better to do with a friend.

PRACTICAL TASK PRACTICAL TASK PRACTICAL TASK PRACTICAL TASK PRACTICAL TASK

Say the word *yes* out loud a few times. Say it as if you really mean it. Now, as you continue to say *yes* out loud, imagine that you are tired of saying *yes* and really want to say no. As you continue to say *yes* out loud, imagine that you are not sure if your answer should be *yes* or *no*. Note how your voice changes as you change the intended meaning.

It's likely that, initially, the word was expressed clearly, your voice upbeat and perhaps a little clipped with a short pause between each repetition. Then, as you thought about wanting to say *no*, your voice would probably have dropped in volume and tone, so that the *yes* expanded and was expressed almost as a pronounced sigh, signalling weariness. As you then thought about whether to say *yes* or *no,* your voice may well have dropped again in volume and gained an extra syllable, the first one rising slightly and the second falling. Alternatively you may have expressed it on a rising tone as a question. At the same time it is likely that the pause between each word lengthened. In this task you have used the pace, tone and volume of your voice to change the meaning of your message.

Paralanguage also includes filler sounds such as *um* and *er*, as well as coughs and laughter. We are more likely to use these filler sounds when we are feeling nervous or we need time to think.

Body language

We have already established that our voice can convey a larger proportion of our message than the words we use, so you probably won't be too surprised to learn that the proportion of our message conveyed through body language can be even higher. This point is delightfully illustrated when we see young students receiving their GCSE and GCE A level results. Their bodies are not talking, but shouting.

Body language includes facial expression, gesture and posture and we'll take each of them in turn.

Facial expression

Do you ever wonder at the complexity of the human face? There are over six billion people in the world, almost all of them with the normal features you would expect to find on a face. Yet, apart from identical twins, no two people look the same. And when you think about it you realise just how well adapted and how infinitely versatile our faces are for expressing the depth and breadth our thoughts and feelings.

PRACTICAL TASK PRACTICAL TASK PRACTICAL TASK PRACTICAL TASK PRACTICAL TASK

Repeat the task on saying *yes*. This time watch yourself in a mirror. Note the expression on your face and identify any changes.

You will notice that the expression on your face will change as you alter the volume, pace and tone of your voice. This task illustrates how we use our facial expression in conjunction with our voice to convey meaning.

It would seem an awesome task to attempt to catalogue the diversity of facial expression. Nevertheless Paul Eckman and Wallace Friesen (1975) have identified six facial expressions that are most easily recognisable. They are anger, disgust, surprise, interest, sadness and happiness.

Friesen and Sorenson (cited in Pease and Pease, 2005) suggest that these facial expressions are universal. This would indicate that some of the features of NVC are unlearned and therefore innate.

Identify the facial expressions.

| 1 | 2 | 3 | 4 | 5 | 6 |

(The answers are at the end of the chapter.)

Two features of facial expression are particularly relevant to us as teachers. These are eye contact and smiling, so let's consider them in a little more detail.

Have you ever sat in a busy place and observed couples around you deep in conversation? You will probably have noticed that each will make frequent eye contact with the other and if the two people happen to be in love, their eye contact is likely to be continuous. What does this eye contact mean? Clearly, for our two lovers it's saying, *You're the most wonderful person in the world*. And in fact, this wouldn't be so far from the truth as a general statement. Returning your eyes to the other person tells them that you think they are worthy of your attention, that they are important to you. and that you value what they are saying. Indeed, when you are listening to someone speaking, making frequent eye contact not only confirms your interest in what they are saying, but also invites them to continue speaking. Argyle's research (1994) into eye contact indicates that when we are in conversation we make eye contact 41% of the time when we are talking but 75% of the time when we are listening. This research shows us the importance of eye contact when listening.

Similarly, it would be difficult to overstate the value of smiling. We seem to be hard wired to respond positively when people smile at us. Interestingly, this is the case even though we are usually unaware of it. So, smiling at learners passes a very positive signal to them that encourages them to respond positively.

When you are next in a classroom take a minute or two to observe the faces of the learners in conversation with each other. Watch how often they smile and the frequency of their eye contact.

Gesture
Gestures can convey complex and powerful meaning quickly and clearly. For example, if you nod appropriately at learners when they are speaking it encourages them to continue because they feel that they are being listened to and that their contributions are valued.

Let's now look at some other gestures.

You notice your learners making the following gestures:

- folding arms in front;
- crossing arms in front as if giving a self hug;
- biting bottom lip;
- raising eyebrows and keeping them raised;
- shrugging shoulders.

What messages do you think are being passed? Note your response and compare with the comments below.

The first three gestures can be signs of discomfort. Folded arms can mean *I don't want to be here* or *I'm bored*. A self-hug and lip biting can mean uncertainty and nervousness. The last two gestures could be seen as aggressive: raised eyebrows can mean *I don't believe what you're saying*, and shrugging, *I don't know* or *I don't care.*

Posture

Our body posture, the way we move, stand or sit, can give those around us information about how we feel.

Look at these three figures (based on Wainwright, 1996). What messages do you think are being passed about how each figure is feeling?

The first figure signals confidence and openness, while the posture of figure two signals sadness or lack of confidence. The final figure could be signalling arrogance or even aggression. This is worth remembering when you are in the classroom. Making sure you stand tall and look up is not difficult, but it makes a real difference to how we are seen by learners.

Proximity, orientation, appearance and touch

Proximity

Proximity refers to the distance we keep between ourselves and others. This distance will vary from culture to culture and from individual to individual. It will also vary from situation to situation. We are likely feel completely comfortable in close proximity to those we know well, but less so with strangers. Have you ever noticed that when people enter a waiting room they often choose the seat that is the furthest away from those who are already seated? If more people enter, this space becomes smaller as the newcomers are forced to fill in the gaps.

Orientation

This is similar to proximity but refers, not to distance, but to our position in relation to others. Sitting face to face, as is usual for an interview, creates a more formal atmosphere than sitting at right-angles. Knapp and Hall's research (1992) into orientation found that sitting at right-angles is probably the best choice to create a positive and comfortable atmosphere.

Appearance

We pass messages to others through our physical appearance. The clothes that you are wearing today will say something about you. The same is true for your choice of hairstyle or your jewellery. All of these choices pass messages about someone who wears a certain make of jeans or who wears clothes for comfort. Sometimes this identity with a certain look becomes more rigid. A good illustration is the style of clothes worn by Goths. Sometimes we change our look in order to change our message. You may well go to an interview in more formal clothes than usual because you want the interviewer to know that you are smart, organised and business-like.

REFLECTIVE TASK

Think about the clothes you would wear in the following teaching situations. Would your choice be different for each of them? Consider the reasons for this.

- HNC in Business and Management.

- An engineering workshop.

- A return to learn programme.

Touch

There are strict cultural and gender rules about touching. It is also true that some of us are more tactile than others, so we have to approach the issue with sensitivity. Having said that, being touched on the arm or hand is unlikely to offend. Perhaps, more importantly, as the following piece of research shows, touching passes a very powerful positive message; it actually makes people feel good.

Wainwright (1996) refers to research at an American university where a library assistant was asked to touch the hands of a proportion of new students as they handed over their new library cards. When the students were asked later to rate the library, including the assistant for friendliness and helpfulness, the proportion of new students that had been touched by the assistant gave higher scores, even those students who had been unaware they had been touched.

The unconscious nature of NVC

Many of the non-verbal messages we give and receive are conscious or deliberate messages. You may, for example, see a friend across the street and, rather than shout *hello*, you wave. You may alter the pace of your voice when in front of a class to give meaning and emphasis to your words and to make the topic interesting. Alternatively you may use a formal method of NVC such as sign language or Makaton. However, much of our NVC is unconscious and to understand why, we need to delve briefly into our past.

We don't really know when human beings first acquired language, but we do know that our automatic responses to our environment are far older. Our instinctive reactions to danger have enabled us to engage in fight or flight in order to survive, and because we have been doing it for such a long time, it is well engrained and we are very good at it. Thankfully, we no longer have to worry about being eaten by a wild animal. We are, however, still able to react instinctively when placed in seemingly threatening situations, as anyone who is frightened of spiders or snakes will confirm. This ancient instinct of flight or fight still influences our behaviour. When we are frightened we give defensive signals. The object of our fears may well have changed but our reactions less so. This is why, when faced with a situation where we feel nervous, for example facing a new class, we may unconsciously cross our arms in front of us as a protection, or we may speak in a rush because we want the situation over and done with as quickly as possible.

Of course, not all of our non-verbal signals are connected to fear. Some people are just naturally expressive, but whether or not we are one of these expressive people, as we grow older, our NVC does become habitual. Our facial expressions, gestures, posture and even the clothes we wear all become part of who we are.

One important aspect of the automatic and habitual nature of NVC is that we are sometimes unaware of the messages we are giving to those around us. A friend of mine who was a teacher for many years would use a chopping motion with his right hand, with the index finger pointing outwards, whenever he made a point.

REFLECTIVE TASK

What do you understand by this gesture? How would it make you feel?

Some of his learners probably didn't even notice his gesture. But some could have understood it as a gesture of authority or even aggression. Indeed, it is unlikely to have made any of them feel good.

Pease and Pease (2005) carried out an experiment with eight lecturers using different hand gestures as they gave identical 10-minute talks to a range of audiences. When the lecturers made hand gestures with the palm facing up, 84% of the audience gave a positive response. When the lecturers used palm-down, finger-pointing gestures, this figure dropped to 28% and some participants walked out before the end. Some of these participants may well have felt uncomfortable without realising why. And this is the rub. Sometimes our NVC can make others feel negative, and they may not even know why they feel the way they do.

We can also make others feel uncomfortable when our words say one thing but our non-verbal signals say something different.

This is more likely to happen when we feel stressed, angry, irritated, worried or tired. Let's have a look at a situation to illustrate this point.

SCENARIO STUDY – BETHAN – MIXED MESSAGES

Beth has set some tasks for her learners to do at home and all of them, apart from Judy, have handed in their work. Beth isn't surprised at this as Judy often hands in work late. When Judy finally hands in her work she tells Beth that she really will get her next piece in on time. Beth's response to this is to raise her eyebrows, look up and take a short intake of breath as she says to Judy, *Of course you will*.

PRACTICAL TASK PRACTICAL TASK PRACTICAL TASK PRACTICAL TASK PRACTICAL TASK

What do you think is happening here? Try to visualise Beth's NVC. Do you think it is in conflict with her words? Is there another message that Beth is passing? How might Judy feel? Note your answers and compare them with the comments below.

Beth is feeling irritated and perhaps a little annoyed because Judy is always late with her work. She may well have already asked Judy to try to get her work in on time. It is likely that if Beth were to say what she really felt she would tell Judy that she was sick and tired of having to mark her work late. All credit to Beth that she isn't openly angry, but her irritation is leaking out, and in this instance it is leaking out as sarcasm. Although her words are confirming a belief that Judy will get her work in on time, her non-verbal signals are saying that she thinks it very unlikely. Judy, on the receiving end of this double message, is likely to feel confused because Beth is passing a contradictory message. She is also likely to feel uncomfortable because sarcasm almost always has this effect.

REFLECTIVE TASK

Consider this. You want to ask something of a colleague. It will only take a minute or two of her time but it is important. When you next see her, you ask her if she has time for a quick word. She says, *yes, of course*, but as you begin to speak, you are conscious that her body is turned a little away from you and her eye contact is fleeting. She may even take a surreptitious glance at her watch. How do you feel? Do you believe her words or her NVC?

Although your colleague has said that she has time to talk, her non-verbal signals are telling you that she really needs to be elsewhere. She may be giving this double message because she feels she ought to stop and talk even though she knows she doesn't have time. You will pick up more meaning from her leaked non-verbal signals than her words and you are likely to feel uncomfortable and confused. Should you continue speaking or tell her you'll catch her another time?

There is some good news about NVC, in fact some very good news. If we sometimes unconsciously use it to make others feel bad, we can certainly use it to make others feel good, to make them feel valued, confident and motivated. And some more good news is that although, initially, it takes a little thought, after a very short time it becomes habitual, automatic, a part of who we are and how others see us.

It is worth taking a look now at a breakdown of the percentage of meaning conveyed through verbal/non-verbal communication.

Words	7%
Paralanguage	38%
Body language	55%

Figure 8.1 How we convey meaning (after Mehrabian, 1971)

Are you surprised that such a small percentage of our message is passed by our words and such a large percentage is communicated non-verbally? I certainly was when I first saw these figures and remember wondering why we put so much energy into words when we have this wonderful tool that we can use to pass powerful messages effortlessly. What an opportunity!

NVC in the classroom

Now let's see how some of the features of NVC are relevant to the classroom. We will look at Ben and his class of BTEC National learners.

SCENARIO STUDY – BEN – SOME NEGATIVE NVC

Ben is a first year PGCE trainee at the start of his course, and he is just about to begin his second lesson with a group of learners on a BTEC National course in business administration. Ben likes his students and he likes his subject, but he is not looking forward to this session because he feels there was something not quite right about the first session. He can't put his finger on what it was. There were no problems with the learners, in fact they were great, and the session went OK, but – and it's a big but – the session was just OK, and Ben feels that it could have been so much better, that somehow it could have been much more enjoyable for the learners and, indeed, for himself.

As Ben enters the room for his second session the learners are sitting in small groups talking fairly quietly amongst themselves. Ben nods at one or two who have made eye contact with him as he enters, and then he goes to sit behind the desk at the front. He is conscious that this session must go really well so he makes sure that his lesson plans on the desk in front of him are all in order, rather than looking up to say good morning.

The session proceeds as before, with the learners listening to Ben and then contributing well to the question and answer session. Ben has planned a discussion topic that he feels the learners will find really interesting, and as each group begins to get into animated debate he is pleased at his choice and the effort he put into planning it. At this point he gets up from behind the desk and wanders around from group to group in case they need any help. He doesn't want to interfere, so he stands behind each group for a few minutes before moving on to the next one. At the end of the session as the learners are leaving, Joe, one of the more confident and chatty members of the class, stops in the doorway. He turns suddenly to Ben and with a big grin says, *Wow, that was a great discussion, but I wish you'd lighten up a bit – you look like you've got the world and his mate on your shoulders*.

PRACTICAL TASK PRACTICAL TASK PRACTICAL TASK PRACTICAL TASK PRACTICAL TASK

How many of Ben's negative non-verbal signals did you spot?

What advice could you give to Ben?

Ben seems to have had a pretty motivated group of learners, and he was perceptive enough to realise that his first lesson wasn't quite right even though he couldn't work out why. Hopefully, Joe's comment got him thinking about the expression on his face and, perhaps also, his posture. Unfortunately, some of us are unlucky enough to have a facial expression that can look a little pained when we are in default mode so it can sometimes take a little effort to look more cheerful. It is much more likely though that Ben's pained look is because he is tense and doesn't find communicating comes naturally. Here are Ben's non-verbal errors.

- He just nods when he enters the room, and only at the learners who make eye contact. This gives the impression that he is not too interested in them. In fact some of the learners may even be unaware that he has entered the room.
- He sits behind the desk cutting himself off from the class.
- He looks at his lesson plan when greeting the learners. This is another separation signal.
- He doesn't smile (assuming Joe's comments are correct). This is a missed opportunity to engage with the learners.
- He stands behind each group. His close proximity could make some of the learners feel uncomfortable.

You could make the following suggestions to Ben.

- He could make sure that everyone knows he has entered the room by greeting the class as soon as he enters, smiling and making eye contact with every learner.
- He could position himself in front of the desk. This would signal confidence and a willingness to be involved with the learners.
- He could try to smile more, especially during the question and answer session, to validate the learners' contributions.
- He could tell the learners to ask for help if they have a problem and then leave them to get on with their discussion.

Now that you have looked at Ben's experience you might find it useful to record in your journal any initial thoughts you have about your own non-verbal signals.

Supporting learners

So, let's now ponder how we can use our knowledge and understanding of NVC in our relationship with our learners. There are two aspects of this relationship that we need to consider in order to make the best possible use of this knowledge. The first is understanding our learners' NVC. The second is being aware of what our NVC is saying to learners.

Understanding our learners' NVC

Because we know that NVC is often automatic and unconscious it follows that learners may not always be aware of the messages they are passing. We know also that NVC will very often convey the very messages that learners may find difficult to articulate, so we can help them when we recognise and understand their non-verbal signals as they communicate with each other and with us. Consider the following two scenarios.

SCENARIO STUDY – THE BTEC NATIONAL GROUP

Six second-year learners on a BTEC National course in Travel and Tourism are engaged in a discussion of a project they are working on together. The group members are sitting together, facing each other, with their bodies leaning forward. The volume of their voices is fairly loud as they discuss the different issues of the topic. As you watch the group, you are aware that the learners' faces are animated and that eye contact within the group is dynamic as the conversation moves around. You also notice that one group member speaks louder, more frequently and for longer than any of the others.

SCENARIO STUDY – THE MOTOR VEHICLE GROUP

Twenty auto technician learners are sitting at desks facing a teacher who is speaking to them. Most of the learners are looking at the teacher most of the time, although one or two are frowning. One learner is looking down at the desk in front of her, another cradles his chin in his hand as he rests his arm on the desk, and two or three are fiddling with bags or pens. The room is quiet and from time to time most of the learners move a little in their seats as they adjust their bodies to a slightly different position.

PRACTICAL TASK PRACTICAL TASK PRACTICAL TASK PRACTICAL TASK PRACTICAL TASK

What could you learn by observing the NVC of these two groups? How would you respond to the NVC of the second group? Note your answers and compare them with the comments below.

The NVC of the BTEC National group shows that they are participating in a fairly heated discussion of their project. All the group members are actively involved and it is likely they will produce a good action plan. However, one group member clearly has difficulty reading the non-verbal signals of the others and the teacher might need to intervene.

The NVC of the motor vehicle group indicates that they are possibly bored and physically uncomfortable. The learners who are frowning may not understand or agree with what is being said. It would be a good idea at this point to change the learners' activity. This may mean introducing some group work or taking a five-minute break to enable them to stand up and move around. It would then be appropriate to give the learners an opportunity to contribute and to ask questions.

Perhaps the most important point we can take from these two scenarios is that we need to be focused on our learners in order to interpret their non-verbal signals. Are they able to read the non-verbal signals of those around them? Are they interested, are they engaged? They may not always tell us that they are worried about something they have been asked to do, or that they don't understand, or that they are bored, but their NVC will often be shouting it loudly and clearly.

Understanding our own NVC

We saw earlier that we have unconscious expressions and gestures that are peculiar to us. They are part of who we are and, of course, the last thing we want to do is to attempt to change something about ourselves that is so personal. Indeed, these personal traits are often viewed with kindly amusement by those around us, including our learners. What we want to do is to make sure that we don't pass messages that our learners might see as negative.

Here are some examples of NVC that you should try to avoid.

• Standing or sitting with your arms folded or crossed in front of you as in a self-hug; this could mean you are feeling tense or uncomfortable.
• Turning your body away during a one-to-one conversation; this could mean you are not interested or don't have time.
• Excessive gestures such as frequent hand chopping or pointing; these could be seen as aggressive.
• Making infrequent eye contact with learners; this could indicate lack of interest.
• Positioning yourself behind a desk; this can convey a desire to be separate.
• Bent shoulders; this can indicate weariness and/or lack of confidence.
• Passing contradictory messages; it can be confusing for learners if our paralanguage and/or our body language conflicts with our words.

If there are some features of NVC we need to avoid, there are certainly many that will help to enthuse our learners and make them feel positive, confident and motivated. Here are some examples of NVC you should try to make part of your personal repertoire.

• Smiling; this doesn't mean becoming a Cheshire cat, but smiling will show learners that you are relaxed and that you enjoy being with them. Smiling will also encourage them to contribute.
• Making eye contact; this goes hand in hand with smiling and shows that you are interested in your learners.
• Nodding agreement when learners contribute; this shows that you are listening and that what they are saying is important and interesting.
• Standing tall and looking at everyone; this signals that you are in charge.
• Changing the pace and tone of your voice; this signals that the topic is interesting and helps to emphasise important points.
• Using open hand gestures with the palm up; this can help emphasise the importance and interest of a topic.

A SUMMARY OF KEY POINTS

> Non-verbal communication includes the way we use our voice, our facial expression, our gestures, posture, appearance, orientation and proximity to others.

> Some features of NVC are universal and appear to be innate.

> Some features of NVC are learned. These may convey different meaning in different cultures.

> Non-verbal communication can be deliberate, as in waving to a friend, or unconscious, for example, avoiding eye contact.

> A greater proportion of the meaning of a message can be conveyed through NVC than though words.

> When there is conflict between our verbal and our non-verbal message it is confusing for the listener and makes them feel uncomfortable.

> It is important to be aware of the non-verbal signals of learners. These may convey discomfort, such as puzzlement or boredom.

> We can use non-verbal signals positively to support speaking, to convey interest and to confirm listening.

> Frequent eye contact and smiling are the two most positive and effective features of non-verbal communication.

Branching options

The following tasks are designed to allow you to consolidate and develop your understanding of NVC.

Reflection

In one of your next classes, try to identify the messages that your learners are sending through their NVC. What impressions did you gain when you walked into the classroom? Did these impressions change during the lesson and was the learners' NVC different at the end of the lesson? Were they enthusiastic, bored, confrontational, respectful or something else? What non-verbal signals can you identify which led you to your conclusions? Where appropriate, make notes in your journal.

Analysis

Try to get yourself videoed in one of your lessons, or observed by a friendly colleague. The aim is to identify features of your own body language. What gestures do you frequently use? Do you smile and nod in agreement? Do you put barriers between yourself and the learners? Try to identify those features of your NVC that are positive and reinforcing, and those that are negative and distracting.

Research

Use the internet or your library to find out more about NVC. How can you apply this to your teaching?

Answers to task on facial expressions:

1. sadness; 2. anger; 3. surprise; 4. interest; 5. disgust; 6. happiness.

REFERENCES AND FURTHER READING REFERENCES AND FURTHER READING

Argyle, M (1994) *The psychology of interpersonal behaviour*. London: Penguin.

Ekman, P and Friesen, WV (1975) *Unmasking the face: a guide to recognizing emotions from facial clues*. Englewood Cliffs, NJ: Prentice-Hall.

Knapp, M and Hall, J (1992) *Non-verbal communication in human interaction*. New York: Holt Rinehart & Winston.

Mehrabian, A (1971) *Silent messages.* Belmont, NY: Wadsworth Publishing Co.

Morris, D (2002) *Bodytalk: A world guide to gestures.* London: Jonathan Cape.

Pease, A and Pease, B (2005) *The definitive book of body language*. London: Orion.

Wainwright, GR (1996) *Teach yourself body language*. London: Hodder & Stoughton.

9
Reading

This chapter will help you to:

- **learn about theories of reading;**
- **understand how they can be applied to develop your own reading skills and those of your learners.**

Links to minimum core elements:
A 2.5   Interpreting written texts.
A 2.6   Knowledge of how textual features support reading.
A 2.7   Understand the barriers to accessing text.
B 6   Find, and select from, a range of reference material and sources of information, including the internet.
B 7   Use and reflect on a range of reading strategies to interpret texts and locate information and meaning.
B 8   Identify and record the key information of messages contained within reading material using note-taking techniques.

Links to LLUK Professional Standards for QTLS:
AS4, AS7, AK5.1, BK2.2, BP2.2, BK3.1, BK3.3, BK3.4, BP3.1, BP3.3, BP3.4, BK5.1, BP5.1, CK3.4, CP3.4.

Links to LLUK mandatory units of assessment:
Planning and enabling learning (CTLLS and DTLLS):

- **understand how to use a range of communication skills and methods to communicate effectively with learners and relevant parties in own organisation;**
- **understand and demonstrate knowledge of the minimum core in own practice.**

Enabling learning and assessment (DTLLS):

- **understand and demonstrate how to give effective feedback to promote learner progress and achievement;**
- **understand and demonstrate knowledge of the minimum core in own practice.**

Theories and principles for planning and enabling learning (DTLLS):

- **understand and demonstrate knowledge of the minimum core in own practice.**

Introduction

I expect you are a fluent reader. You probably wouldn't be reading this book or be involved in the teaching profession unless you were. I expect, too, that you're not aware of how you go about reading. Like the majority of fluent readers, it's just something you are able to do, and you do it automatically. Yet reading is not a natural gift that we are born with; it is a skill that we learn. As a fluent reader you probably learned your reading skills a long time ago with little idea of how you did it, or how you continue to be able to read and understand and learn from your reading.

This chapter begins by focusing on the reading process. It provides insight into how we give meaning to the shapes on a page or screen in front of us. It will give you some techniques for developing your own reading skills and suggest ways in which you can support your learners as they develop their reading skills.

The reading process

Smith (1978) suggests that any one definition of reading, for example, *decoding of written word into sound*, is not adequate to describe its range and diversity. It might therefore be more useful here to use a fairly general statement and say that reading is about understanding the written word. Even this has its problems. What do we actually mean by understanding? Let me explain. I know that Spanish is spoken more or less as it is written, so I could read a Spanish newspaper. Nevertheless, if I were to read one out loud, a fluent Spanish speaker might understand most of it but I would understand very little. So, we can't honestly say that reading words correctly is understanding.

We have another problem with the word *understanding*. Suppose you decide to read a technical manual on a subject you know little about and that you understand the meaning of, say, 90 per cent of the words. Would you say this was understanding? Would you have understood the meaning of the manual in the way the writer intended you should? Perhaps we could say that understanding is when we are able to learn from our reading and are able to communicate it to others. This has relevance for us in our professional life and it applies whether we are reading for our own assignments or to research material to use with our learners.

So how do we do it? What is the process that allows us to sort the squiggly shapes in front of us into a pattern that makes sense to us? Psychologists tell us that although it begins with our visual perception, it is our brain that interprets the shapes and patterns as letters and words (Woods, 2004). The process is not passive; words don't just jump from the page into our heads. Just like speaking and listening, we are actively involved in constructing meaning from these shapes. Theories or models of reading provide a starting point for an examination of how this happens.

A reading model tries to depict how an individual perceives a word, processes a clause and comprehends a text (Ruddell and Singer, 1985). Most reading models come in one of two versions, different only in their approach to the process. In version one, referred to as a top-down approach, understanding begins with the knowledge and experience of the reader. In version two, referred to as a bottom-up approach, understanding begins with the written text itself. Let's look at these two models to see what they can tell us.

Top-down reading models

Top-down models suggest our understanding of written text begins with the knowledge that we bring to reading. We use this knowledge to interpret the text in a way that is meaningful to us.

PRACTICAL TASK PRACTICAL TASK PRACTICAL TASK PRACTICAL TASK PRACTICAL TASK

Consider the following newspaper headlines:

BRITISH LEFT WAFFLES ON FALKLAND ISLANDS
FARMER BILL DIES IN HOUSE
SAFETY EXPERTS SAY SCHOOL BUS PASSENGERS SHOULD BE BELTED

What would you say is the writer's intended meaning for each of these headlines? What knowledge or experience enabled you to interpret these headlines as the writer intended? What other interpretation is there?

You probably had little trouble in understanding the headlines because you know that *left* refers to the British Labour Party, and *house* refers to one of the houses of parliament and so on. But there is an important point here. As we can see from this task, knowledge will often be culturally and experientially specific.

Context also plays an important role in our understanding of written language. We can include here both the physical context i.e., where you are when you are reading, and the medium or artefact, for example, letter or computer screen, which carries the message.

PRACTICAL TASK PRACTICAL TASK PRACTICAL TASK PRACTICAL TASK PRACTICAL TASK

Look at the following statement:

The Red Brigade returns!

What would it mean to you if:

• you were reading a thriller set in Italy in the late 1970s?
• you were reading the local newspaper in Liverpool?
• you saw it on a hoarding at a local by-election?

You may well already know about Italian terrorist groups in the 1970s, you may be a football fan and you may be familiar with the concept of red to indicate extreme left-wing politics, but the context will have helped to guide you towards the appropriate interpretation.

There are important points to be learnt from top-down reading models.

• Learners have a range of cultural and experiential backgrounds that they bring to their interpretation of written text. This is important for preparing handouts; don't assume that everyone will interpret them in the way you intend.
• Learners bring specific knowledge and experience to their reading. The chances are that they will already have knowledge related to their current learning. Tap in to that knowledge in the classroom, by giving opportunities for learners to express it, and use it to guide your choice of appropriate reading for them.

Bottom-up reading models

Bottom-up models suggest that our understanding of written language develops from learning to decode its rules. We focus on the sounds of the alphabet and the smallest units, or phonemes, such as *ou* and *ee,* then words and then sentences. Textual features, including spelling, punctuation and grammar, play an important role in helping us to interpret text by providing clues to its meaning. Cornbleet and Carter (2001) refer to a number of textual features or sub-skills of writing, and it is useful for us to look briefly at some of them now and the way in which they support the text.

Spelling

For the most part spelling follows a set of conventions. We know what to expect when we see the letters *ing* together even though the setting might be different. There are specific spelling rules too, for example, *i before e, except after c*, which apply in the majority of instances.

Punctuation

Similarly, punctuation follows a set of conventions: we know, for example, that a comma indicates a pause and a full stop indicates the end of a specific thought.

Grammar

Grammatical rules have an important role in understanding. One example is the rule relating to word order. In the English language the order is subject, verb, object, *I kicked the ball*, and definite article, adjective, noun, *the red car*.

PRACTICAL TASK PRACTICAL TASK PRACTICAL TASK PRACTICAL TASK PRACTICAL TASK

Read the following sentence:

> *Two and coffees a please doughnut.*

What is the correct word order for this sentence to make sense?

It doesn't make sense as it is because the words are in the wrong order, but it probably took you only a second or two to realise that the sentence should read *two coffees and a doughnut please.* This is because you know the rules of how words relate to each other and can predict the meaning of the sentence.

Style

We read text in a whole range of different styles. Compare an academic style, which has an extensive vocabulary and complex sentences, with a children's style, which has a restricted vocabulary and simple sentences.

Format

There is a considerable range of text format which you will come across in your reading and which you can choose from when writing. For example, if you decided to contact a friend you might choose to send a conventional letter, an email or a text message on a mobile phone. The format would be different for each of these. In your letter you would probably begin with *dear* or *hello*, use sentences and finish with *love from* or *write soon*. Your email would omit the opening, use short phrases and sign off with your name. In your text message you are likely to use an abbreviated language code.

Visual image

Text can be accompanied by visual images that support and reinforce its meaning. For example, advertisers will often use strong visual images to reinforce the text in order to sell their products. Visual image, style and format can also indicate intended audience and purpose.

PRACTICAL TASK PRACTICAL TASK PRACTICAL TASK PRACTICAL TASK PRACTICAL TASK

Read this flyer aimed at people who have been out of the workforce because of childcare responsibilities.

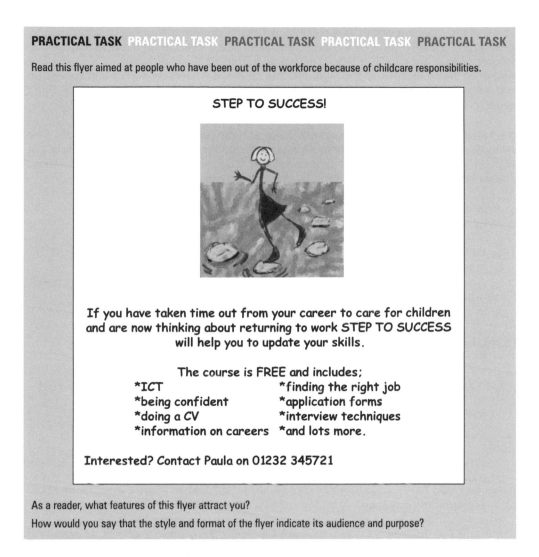

STEP TO SUCCESS!

If you have taken time out from your career to care for children and are now thinking about returning to work STEP TO SUCCESS will help you to update your skills.

The course is FREE and includes;
*ICT   *finding the right job
*being confident   *application forms
*doing a CV   *interview techniques
*information on careers *and lots more.

Interested? Contact Paula on 01232 345721

As a reader, what features of this flyer attract you?

How would you say that the style and format of the flyer indicate its audience and purpose?

You might have said that the picture of the smiling young woman, walking determinedly across stepping-stones, supports the text in aiming at a youngish, female audience and indicating stepping successfully into a job. You might also have felt that the use of a first name only for the telephone contact and an informal font style might indicate a welcoming and friendly approach.

Rhythm and pattern

REFLECTIVE TASK

Consider this verse from a poem by Robert Louis Stevenson:

Faster than fairies, faster than witches,
Bridges and houses, hedges and ditches;
And charging along like troops in a battle,
All through the meadows the horses and cattle;
Fly as thick as driving rain;
And ever again, in the wink of an eye,
Painted stations whistle by.

Some of the meaning of this text is conveyed by its rhythm. It's not difficult to imagine looking out of the window of a train as it speeds along even though the strongest clue doesn't appear until the last line. (The poem is entitled *From a Railway Carriage.*) The rhythm of the poem reflects the rhythm of the sound of wheels on a track and speeds up as the train accelerates. Try reading it aloud, imagining the rhythm of a steam train. Don't forget to speed up.

We become accustomed to the textual rules and conventions of written English. One example, which we have already looked at, is the pattern of word order. But this is not necessarily the same in other languages. Look at how the word order of these sentences changes when translated into French, German and Spanish.

Janet likes red wine.
Janet aime le vin rouge (Janet likes wine red).

So I would like to buy her a bottle.
So möchte ich eine Flasche kaufen (So would like I (for) her a bottle to buy).

I will give it to her tomorrow.
Te lo daré mañana (To her it I will give tomorrow).

Textual context

PRACTICAL TASK PRACTICAL TASK PRACTICAL TASK PRACTICAL TASK PRACTICAL TASK PRACTICAL TASK

Complete the following sentence:

If ___ can read ____ sentence, you will see ____ you don't need __ read ___ words __ order ___ it to ____ sense.

In this task you have used the context provided by the text to make assumptions about the meaning of the sentence.

Bottom-up approaches provide important learning points when it comes to preparing reading materials such as handouts and PowerPoint presentations. Learners use the clues provided by textual features and context to help them interpret the text.

We therefore need to make sure that:

- handouts and presentations are clear and unambiguous;
- the style and format are appropriate for all of the learners;
- spelling, punctuation and grammar are correct;
- we use visual images when appropriate.

We will look at handouts, presentations, style and format in more detail in the section on helping learners to develop their reading skills. Spelling, punctuation and grammar are the subject of Chapter 11.

In reality we use both bottom-up and top-down approaches to reading. If you have ever listened to a small child learning to read, you will have noticed that they will sometimes replace a word in the sentence with a completely different one in terms of its sound and sight, but a word that means exactly the same and makes complete sense in the context of the sentence. They might, for example, replace the word *sleepy* with *tired*, or *large* with *big*. They haven't identified the word in front of them but they have identified its meaning and they have used their knowledge and experience, as well as their understanding of textual context and features, in order to do it.

Developing your reading skills

Some books are to be tasted, others to be swallowed, and some few to be chewed and digested: that is, some books are to be read only in parts; others to be read, but not curiously: and some few to be read wholly and with diligence and attention.
(Francis Bacon, 1561–1626, cited: Adult Literacy Core Curriculum, DfES, 2001)

We read novels, textbooks, letters, journals, manuals, newspaper articles, magazine articles, advertisements, computer screens, mobile phone screens, TV guides, leaflets, posters, safety instructions, medicine bottles, menus, recipes, food labels, washing instruction labels, DVD labels, road maps, road signs, shop signs, directions, street names, logos, headlines, italics, small writing, handwriting, text messages, music (some of us) and so on.

REFLECTIVE TASK

Look again at the list of things we read. Imagine not being able to read any of them. How do you think this would affect your life?

In developing your reading skills there are some specific points worth bearing in mind to make your reading more effective. These are, the reason or purpose of your reading, your reading technique and your note-making technique. We can look at these in more detail.

Reading and purpose

If we try to imagine life without being able to read, as you did in the reflective task above, we might say that the purpose of reading is connected with negotiating our way around our very complex world. However, with such a range and variety of reading material, clearly one catch-all purpose is not going to work. A better approach might be to pinpoint a number of specific purposes for reading.

- We read to find an answer to a question. How long will this meal take to cook in the microwave? What is the weather forecast for tomorrow?
- We read to learn something. We might read to learn about the life cycle of the anopheles mosquito, or learn the lines of a poem or a play.
- We read for pleasure. Most of us will enjoy reading a good novel or an interesting magazine or journal article. We also enjoy maintaining contact with others although emails and text messaging have, to some extent, replaced traditional letter writing.

Clearly, there are many reasons or purposes for reading so it is important to have a clear idea of your purpose. This will save you unnecessary time and effort. What do you want from your reading material? Do you have specific questions you need to find answers to or are you reading for background around a subject area? How much information do you need; sufficient for a detailed assignment or just enough to give a brief report? Armed with this information the task becomes more manageable, although there are still many choices to be made in order to find and select what you need from the extensive range of reading material on offer.

PRACTICAL TASK PRACTICAL TASK PRACTICAL TASK PRACTICAL TASK PRACTICAL TASK

Make a list of the key points you would give to learners on how to research information on projects or assignments. Compare your answers with the list below.

Your list could include the following suggestions:

- How to access and use the library catalogue, including topic searches, author searches and title searches.
- How to search for books on the shelves, i.e., knowledge of the referencing system, for example, Dewey.
- How to use a computer to access the internet or your organisation's intranet.
- How to use Google or other search tools, including techniques to phrase effective queries when entering words in the search box.
- How to use indexes and tables of contents to find specific information in relevant books.
- Where to find periodicals and journals.
- Using the knowledge and experience of the library staff.

Reading techniques

Not everything you read will be of use to you. Knowing what you want from your reading will help you to decide which of the following reading techniques to use.

Scanning
You might scan a telephone directory. It is a useful technique when you need to find a key word or phrase quickly to see if it is relevant to your task. The best way to scan is to read the introduction or the first or last paragraphs of a chapter. Concluding chapters and indexes are also useful.

Skimming
Skim read if you want to get the gist of a text. Move your eyes quickly over the page, ignoring detail and concentrating on identifying the main points. Look at the layout of the text, key words, headings, titles and any illustrations to see if you want to read it in detail.

There are occasions when it is useful to read quickly. The way to increase your reading speed is not by moving your eyes across the page more quickly but by increasing the span of your eyes. You can easily learn to recognise four or five words in a single eye span. Try the following method.

- Imagine the page in front of you divided vertically into three equal sections.
- As you read, concentrate on moving your eyes, not along the line, but from section to section.
- When you feel comfortable, reduce the sections to two per page.

Detailed or active reading
This is careful reading, when you become involved with the text and take time to read every word to make sure you understand its meaning.

- Decide what you want from your reading; set goals, for example, *I want to look at* …
- Keep a dictionary with you and look up any words you don't understand as soon as

you see them.

- Start by skimming the text to get the general idea.
- Take notice of any graphs, charts or illustrations that might help convey the meaning of the text.
- Try to identify sequences in the text that can help you navigate your way around, for example, *there are a number of reasons why* … will indicate that a number of points will follow.
- Read a few sentences or a paragraph then try to sum up what you've read without looking at the text.
- Reread to find answers to specific questions.
- Reread difficult bits.
- When possible use highlighters to identify important key points.
- Afterwards, try to think aloud or explain what you've read to someone else.

Critical reading

To read critically you must be prepared not to accept what you read at face value but to approach it with an open and questioning mind. Nor should you be afraid of challenging any assumptions made. In any event, be aware of the writer's political, religious or cultural background.

PRACTICAL TASK PRACTICAL TASK PRACTICAL TASK PRACTICAL TASK PRACTICAL TASK

Select an issue that is currently in the headlines. Compare the way the issue is reported in a tabloid newspaper such as the *Sun* with that of a broadsheet such as the *Daily Telegraph*. How does the reporting differ for each article? Would you say that the writing takes a particular standpoint or has a hidden agenda based on the writer's own viewpoint?

Reading and note-making techniques

You will often need to remember the key points of your reading and the best way to do this is to make notes or diagrams. If you want your notes to be effective you must have a focus. If you are clear about their purpose you'll save time and produce notes that are organised and relevant. Here are some tips for effective note-making.

- Have your project or assignment brief with you to focus your thoughts.
- Make sure that the text is relevant; use skimming and scanning techniques to check.
- Record bibliography details, i.e., author, date, etc. first; it's easy to forget to do this later.
- Make a note of chapter and page number in case you need to check back later.
- Be clear when copying direct quotes; highlight to show that it is a quote and always note the source.
- Write your notes using your own words; this will help to ensure that you have understood what you have written.
- Use your own abbreviations.

There are a number of ways you can organise your notes and it is really up to you to decide which one suits you. Here are three options; it's worth trying them all to see how you feel or you might want to use them in combination.

Linear notes

This is the traditional way of making notes that you probably already know pretty well. You might find it less time-consuming to record your notes as bulleted points rather than sentences.

Spiders and mind maps

These are similar. Spiders place the major theme or idea in the centre of the page with related points working outwards. Figure 9.1 shows a spider for making notes.

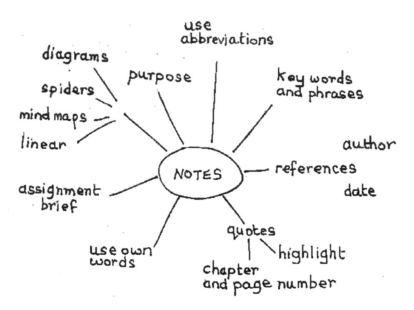

Figure 9.1 A spider diagram

Mind maps are more visual than spider diagrams. You jot down your ideas and link them together in much the same way as your mind makes links between different ideas (see Buzan, 2001). Figure 9.2 shows a mind map on reading techniques.

Diagrams

It's often much easier and quicker to draw a diagram to explain something than to write it. Think about giving directions to a lost driver. If you happened to have a pen and scrap of paper, you wouldn't write *turn left at lights, go on to end of road*. You would draw a map. When you are reading just keep in mind that some things can be explained better with a diagram.

Supporting learners

We know that reading offers us many rich and diverse experiences, and we want our learners to share them. We can help them to develop their reading skills by giving them reading material that is appropriate to their needs and inspires and enthuses them. We can also create situations that will help develop their reading skills by being prepared to take advantage of every opportunity that presents itself. Let's look at a situation where a teacher has not taken advantage of the opportunities to help his learners develop their reading skills.

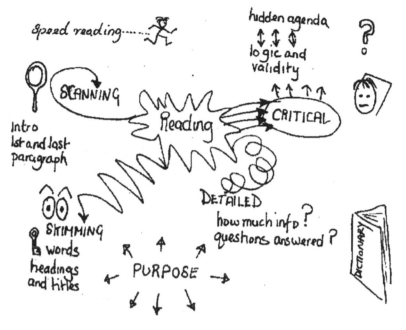

Figure 9.2 A mind map

SCENARIO STUDY – THE ARCHAEOLOGY CLASS

Jack and his friend Tibor are attending the first session of *An Introduction to Archaeology* at the local school. Neither of them knows anything about archaeology but they are very keen and the leaflet says Beginners welcome, so here they are.

The teacher works his way through all the preliminary bits and pieces and then hands round some sheets of paper. He tells the class that he will talk about bronze axes as they are of local interest (quite a few axe heads have been dug up by local farmers over the years) and they can use the information sheet to refer to anything they don't understand.

After the tea break the teacher hands out some question sheets and suggests that they all have a go at answering the questions using the information sheet to find the answers. Jack studies the first question and looks at the information sheet. It is hard work. For a start, the information sheet is blurred and the typing so small that it's quite difficult to read. It doesn't look interesting or inviting either, as it is just a lot of dense writing. But it isn't just that; it looks like the teacher has photocopied the sheet from an archaeology textbook, the language is unfamiliar and contains a number of words Jack hasn't seen before. He's a pretty good reader but he's struggling to understand what it all means. Goodness knows how Tibor was getting on. Tibor is from Slovakia and is fluent in both Slovak and Hungarian with a good understanding of German, but English is his fourth language after all.

Jack feels disappointed as he and Tibor leave the class, and he changes his mind about getting some archaeology books from the library. Archaeology doesn't appear to be anywhere near as interesting as he thought it would be and the teacher hasn't even asked about the bronze axe head that has been burning a hole in his pocket all evening.

PRACTICAL TASK PRACTICAL TASK PRACTICAL TASK PRACTICAL TASK PRACTICAL TASK

What advice would you give to this archaeology teacher? Make notes and compare them with the comments below.

As teachers we need to be using strategies that provide opportunities for learners to read, and we certainly need to be giving them material that encourages them to read rather than putting them off. A number of strategies aimed at supporting learners have been set out in the companion guide and we'll look at them now to see how their implementation could give Jack and Tibor a different experience.

Use readable, accessible texts

The handouts in this class weren't readable and they weren't accessible. The language was in an academic style that included a number of technical words.

The teacher could:

- adapt the text for the class by rewriting it in a style more suitable for beginners;
- use straightforward language that explains the technical terms;
- use short active sentences;
- use clear headings and bullet points;
- use diagrams to explain some of the points;
- use a typeface of 12pt minimum and a clear font such as Arial or Times;
- use clear unambiguous instructions on the worksheet.

Stimulate prior knowledge before reading

There are many activities the teacher could use to stimulate prior knowledge. He could begin the session by asking the learners about their interest in archaeology. This would also have served as a good ice-breaking exercise. The learners could work in pairs, taking turns to ask each other questions, or in small groups, feeding answers back to the whole class. These activities would increase the learners' understanding of the handout and worksheet and would have been immensely helpful for Tibor. They would also provide an opportunity for the learners to demonstrate their existing knowledge of archaeology. Jack would even get an opportunity to show off his axe head.

Write up new terms and key words

The teacher could write key words and technical terms on the board and explain what they mean. This strategy would also provide an opportunity for the learners to ask about particular words they do not understand; again, of considerable help to Tibor.

Read handouts and other written material

The teacher could read the main points of the handout and worksheet aloud, explaining the technical terms. The learners would then find it easier to engage with the reading material when they complete the worksheet. It would also give them a chance to highlight keywords on their handouts and to add their own notes.

Reinforce written materials with visuals

The teacher could show some pictures or slides of some of the bronze axe heads. It would be even better if he were to acquire a couple of axe heads for the learners to look at and touch.

Your choice of style and format for handouts and presentations may be more significant than it appears initially, and deciding what is appropriate is not that easy. There is a massive and bewildering array of typographical styles available to you. Not only can you choose from a menu of dozens of fonts, but also you can choose italic or bold styles, and any colour or size of lettering you want. So how do you make your choice?

PRACTICAL TASK PRACTICAL TASK PRACTICAL TASK PRACTICAL TASK PRACTICAL TASK

You are the course tutor for an introductory computing course to be run in the local Adult Education Centre. The target audience is adults who want to learn about computing in their leisure time. Here are some contrasting font styles:

Introduction to Computing	Times New Roman
Introduction to Computing	Arial
Introduction to Computing	Courier
Introduction to Computing	Braggadocio
Introduction to Computing	Lucida Blackletter
Introduction to Computing	Bradley Hand
Introduction to Computing	Comic Sans MS

Identify which of these fonts, if any, you would choose for the following purposes, and note the reasons behind your choice:

- **handouts to your learners;**
- **A4-size flyer for the course;**
- **PowerPoint presentations;**
- **a notice directing learners to the classroom.**

Are there any other fonts on your computer that would be better suited than those suggested above?

There is no correct answer to this task. The learning point is to be sensitive to the fact that use of different fonts and typographical styles can significantly affect how your learners approach the material you give them to read. Here are some general guidelines that may help you make the best decision for your particular purpose.

- A serif font, where the letters have little feet (serifs), is very easy to read in large blocks of text. Times New Roman is an example of this.
- A sans-serif font (without serifs) such as Arial stands out in headlines and titles. Also, sans-serif fonts look better online, in websites, emails, and HTML newsletters.
- Mono-spaced fonts, where each letter takes the same amount of space (see Courier above), are probably not as easy to read as proportional typefaces like Times New Roman.
- Decorative fonts, such as Braggadocio and Lucida Blackletter, can be eye-catching and therefore useful in publicity material, but can be tricky to read.
- Fonts such as Comic Sans MS or Bradley-Hand, which mimic handwriting, are more informal and convey a friendly approach.

A SUMMARY OF KEY POINTS

> We use top-down approaches (background knowledge, experience and context) and bottom-up approaches (textual context and features) to interpret text.

> Techniques such as skimming, scanning, detailed or active reading and critical reading help develop effective reading skills.

> Note-making techniques such as linear notes, spiders, mind maps and diagrams are useful for organising information and help consolidate learning.

> The purpose of a piece of text and its intended audience will influence its language style, vocabulary and format.

> We can help learners to develop their reading skills when:

  – our handouts and presentations are easily readable, appropriate for the learners, attractive and with correct spelling, punctuation and grammar;

  – we use techniques such as writing up key words on the board and, where appropriate, diagrams to explain key points and concepts;

  – we use opportunities such as group and class discussion to stimulate prior knowledge.

Branching options

The following tasks are designed to help you consolidate and develop your reading skills and those of your learners.

Reflection

Review the handouts and presentations that you are currently using and, in the light of your understanding of typography, consider whether you have used the most appropriate fonts for the relevant learning situation.

Analysis

Identify ways in which you can ensure that your learners understand and assimilate the material they read. Note your conclusions in your journal.

Research

Research the main characteristics of top-down and bottom-up models of reading. Evaluate these in the context of which model is most appropriate to inform your own teaching.

REFERENCES AND FURTHER READING REFERENCES AND FURTHER READING

Blake, N and Moorhead, J (1993) *Introduction to English language*. London: Macmillan.

Buzan, T (2001) *Head strong*. London: Thorsons.

Carter, R, Goddard, A, Reah, D, Sanger, K and Bowring, M. (2001) *Working with text*. 2nd edn. London: Routledge.

Cornbleet, S and Carter, R (2001) *The language of speech and writing*. London: Routledge.

Cottrell, S (2003) *The study skills handbook*. Basingstoke: Palgrave Macmillan.

Crystal, D (2002) *The English language*. London: Penguin.

LLUK (November 2007) *Inclusive learning approaches for literacy, language, numeracy and ICT*. London: LLUK. (the companion guide).

Ruddell, R, Ruddell, M and Singer, H (1994) *Theoretical models and processes of reading.* Newark, DE: International Reading Association.

Smith, F (1978) *Reading*. Cambridge: Cambridge University Press.

10
Writing

This chapter will help you to:

- **examine the process of writing;**
- **consider how this can be applied to develop your own writing skills and those of your learners.**

Links to minimum core elements:

A 2.8   Communicating the written process.

A 2.9   Using genre to develop writing.

B 9   Write fluently, accurately and legibly on a range of topics.

B 10   Select appropriate format and style of writing for different purposes and different readers.

B 11   Use and reflect on a range of reading strategies to interpret texts and locate information and meaning.

B 12   Understand and use the conventions of grammar consistently when producing written text.

Links to LLUK Professional Standards for QTLS:
AS4, AS7, AK5.1, BK2.2, BP2.2, BK3.1, BK3.3, BK3.4, BP3.1, BP3.3, BP3.4. BK5.1, BP5.1, CK3.4, CP3.4.

Links to LLUK mandatory units of assessment:
Planning and enabling learning (CTLLS and DTLLS):

- **understand how to use a range of communication skills and methods to communicate effectively with learners and relevant parties in own organisation;**
- **understand and demonstrate knowledge of the minimum core in own practice.**

Enabling learning and assessment (DTLLS):

- **understand and demonstrate how to give effective feedback to promote learner progress and achievement;**
- **understand and demonstrate knowledge of the minimum core in own practice.**

Theories and principles for planning and enabling learning (DTLLS):

- **understand and demonstrate knowledge of the minimum core in own practice.**

Introduction

How would you describe something that is well written? Anyone who belongs to a reading group will tell you that an appreciation of a piece of text is subjective. Nevertheless, I would describe the following extract from *To Reach the Clouds* by Philippe Petit as well written.

The gods in my feet know how not to hit the cable, how not to make it move when each foot lands. How do they know? They worked that out during their endless days of rehearsals. They know the slightest addition to the vivacious dance of the catenary curve would mean peril for the wirewalker. They ask the feet to land on the steel rope in such a way that the impact of each step absorbs the swaying of the cable, its vertical oscillations, and its twisting along the axis of the walk; the feet answer by being gentle and understanding, by conversing with the wire-rope, by enticing the huffing and puffing living entity above them to let go of his rage to control. Wirewalker, trust your feet! Let them lead you; they know the way.

(Petit, 2002, p167)

In this extract Petit is describing how he walked a high wire between the twin towers of the New York World Trade Center. The author is writing about the very practical, may I say, mundane subject of putting one foot carefully in front of the other, even though it does take place at some considerable height. Yet, he is able to draw you in so that you want to carry on reading. He uses repeating word patterns, *know how not to ... how not to ...* which mimic the action of one foot being placed in front of another. His choice of words and his writing style convey both the unhurried, measured progression along the wire and exhilaration and wonder of being high above the earth.

Writing well is something we can all achieve provided we are prepared to learn the skills and are prepared to write. This chapter will begin by looking at some features of writing; it will then examine some of the criteria for effective writing to enable you to develop your own writing skills and those of your learners.

Some features of writing

We have a number of ways to describe writing that can help to clarify our understanding of what it means.

Writing means shapes on a page

Of course, we think immediately of written English, a series of words, written in the Roman alphabet, which travel from left to right across the page of a book or a computer screen. This may seem a statement of the obvious but this layout isn't universal. In Arabic, the writing is read from right to left; in Chinese, words are represented by characters known as pictographs and ideographs; in Russian, the Cyrillic alphabet is used.

صفحة عبر السفر التي الأشكال هي الكتابة

写作是形状，穿越页

Сочинение формы которых путешествие по странице

The statements all mean the same thing but do not conform to the conventions of written English. Although for our purposes, words written in the Roman alphabet from left to right across the page is the norm, we should be aware that for some learners this isn't so.

Writing is permanent

In contrast to speaking, writing is permanent over time; this can mean days, years or even generations. The implications of this are huge. Consider, for instance, written law or the writings of religious, cultural or political figures such as Karl Marx. You might also want to contemplate the impact of a writer such as JK Rowling on a whole generation of children.

Writing is distant

The author of a piece of text doesn't need to be face to face with the reader. This brings the obvious advantage *of reliable verbal communication in lengthy and complex statements* (Finnegan, 1975, p81). The written word is vital to communication even in an age where ICT has transformed the process. Indeed, ICT is providing us with a new experience. We are now able to *chat* on the internet; in other words, to engage in the immediate responses of conversation using the written word in the form of emails.

Writing has a formal structure

Writing has a formal structure involving sentences and paragraphs. The meaning is conveyed by textual features such as punctuation. Of course, not all writing is formal; think about the note you leave on the kitchen table as a reminder to get some more bread, or the text message you send to say you'll be a few minutes late.

Writing is purpose-led

You may write to instruct, to inform, to entertain or to influence or persuade others. You have a choice of methods: letters, emails, shopping lists, reports and so on. The purpose of a piece of text will influence the way it is written. Birthday greetings to a friend, for instance, require a completely different medium, style and format from a job application.

REFLECTIVE TASK

Consider how the style and format differ in a poem, an advertisement and a CV. How do you think that the purpose of each will influence the style and format?

Criteria for effective writing

We are exposed to such a multiplicity of writing styles and formats that it can be difficult to identify precisely what it is that makes a particular piece of writing effective. Nevertheless, let's make an attempt.

Many years ago, when I was studying communication theory I learned that all communication should be *clear, concise, correct, complete* and *convincing*. Since then I've seen lists that additionally include *consistent, coherent, coordinated* and *courteous*. I am going to use the first four of the original five plus *consistent* and *coherent* as a format for any piece of effective writing.

Writing should be clear

- Use straightforward phrasing: for example, *it is* ..., rather than, *it would seem to be the case that* ... .
- Avoid ambiguous phrases. The following example is from a newspaper headline: *Panda mating fails; vet takes over*.
- Avoid tautology: for example, *it was totally unique*, or *please re-write this again*.
- Use a clear font when keyboarding.
- Take care when handwriting; make sure it is legible.

Writing should be concise

- Include only information that is relevant even if this means rejecting chunks that are interesting.
- Use bullet points instead of sentences when appropriate.
- Avoid meaningless phrases, for example, *it should be noted that* ... .
- Avoid excessive use of redundant words: for example, *extremely evil*.
- Be ruthless when editing.

Writing should be correct

- Use correct spelling, punctuation and grammar (see next chapter).
- Check that the content is accurate.
- Make sure that any references are correct and that you have copied and referenced direct quotes accurately.

Writing should be consistent

- Use the same textual features, such as language, style and format, throughout your writing.
- Use the same terms throughout: for example, if you use the term *worksheet*, don't later refer to the same thing as a *handout*.

Writing should be coherent

- Use key words and phrases such as *I have written that*... and *now*... to signpost related themes and indicate where you are leading the reader.
- Use headings and subheadings where appropriate.
- Be sure that the overall meaning of your writing makes sense.

Writing should be complete

- Don't leave out any important or relevant information.
- Don't leave information gaps that might affect understanding.

Developing your writing skills

As a trainee working towards QTLS you will be writing essays, assignments and project reports as well as keeping a continuing professional development journal. As a teacher you will be writing schemes of work, lesson plans, handouts and PowerPoint presentations; in addition, you will be giving written feedback to learners. For the purposes of developing writing skills we will look at:

- the writing process;
- writing an essay;
- writing for a project or assignment;
- reflective and evaluative writing;
- writing for learners.

The writing process

We have established that the purpose and audience of a piece of writing will influence the way it is written, so before you tackle any piece of writing you will need to be clear what you want it to achieve, and who you are writing it for. You can then think about how you are going to get started.

Few people can just sit down and write. Most of us need to work hard to produce anything reasonable. The starting point is a plan that has a structure appropriate to the format you are using. For example, the structure for a formal report differs from that of an essay. This is covered in more detail in the next sections.

Most extended writing is structured using paragraphs. These normally have an internal structure of their own and this will be reflected in your overall plan. Typically, a paragraph will incorporate a key sentence that summarises the theme of the paragraph, and illustrative sentences that expand and evidence this theme. If you are giving an opinion, this will normally be stated in your key sentence. The illustrative sentences will contain the facts that justify this opinion, to convince the reader that your view is well founded. Often, a summarising sentence is used to close the paragraph.

Your plan will identify the content and the order in which it will be placed in your chosen format. Now you can work towards producing a first draft. Once completed, go through it carefully using the criteria for effective writing to improve, develop and refine it. It may take a number of drafts before you are happy. When you are writing your first draft you are working at getting important points down on paper and you have to use the words that come to you. As you read through your work you can think about the words and phrases you have used: would other words and phrases be more suitable, would they convey the meaning more accurately or give the sentence a better feel? You may need to read over your work several times and to step back and approach it as if for the first time. It's often helpful at this stage to ask someone else to read it and give you feedback.

Writing an essay

What type of essay do you need to write? Fairbairn and Winch (1993) refer to essays that describe, discuss or evaluate. A descriptive essay is the simplest; you need only to describe an event or concept. A discussion essay is more complex and will probably ask you to interpret, compare and justify. An evaluation essay will require you to be constructively critical and make judgements convincingly backed up by evidence.

Your essay should have a three-part structure. An introduction should show the reader that you understand the key issues and indicate how you are going to answer the question. The main body of your essay will be divided into paragraphs, each of which will express one main point or aspect. Your final paragraph will be your conclusion. Your essay could look something like this.

Introduction	Define some of the key words of the title. Indicate the structure, e.g. *I begin by ... In the following section ... Finally ...*
Each paragraph	Indicate the main point of the paragraph. Provide, and comment on, supporting evidence. Link to the following paragraph.
Conclusion	Show you have answered the question. Summarise the main points of the essay. Make an overall evaluation of the arguments and issues.

Writing for a project or assignment

Extended pieces of writing, say 2000 words or more, are given a variety of names in the context of education and training. Projects, assignments and reports are some of the more commonly used terms, but they mean much the same thing. Writing for a project or assignment isn't too different from the writing you will do in your teaching. In both cases you will gather, organise and present information, so one is good practice for the other. You will obviously already have your course handbook and briefing sheets and these need to be followed diligently.

So how do you begin? Unless you have been given a topic title, your first consideration is the focus of your assignment. It's a good idea to jot down possible topic ideas in your journal as they occur to you. Talking over your ideas with friends and colleagues is also helpful. Once you have a clear idea of your topic you need to gather your thoughts together and put them down on paper. Keywords, spiders and mind maps work well at this stage.

Before you begin writing:

- make an action plan outlining what you intend to achieve by a set date. A grid system works well; you can write your objectives down the left-hand side and your dates along the top. It is immensely satisfying ticking off each objective as you achieve it, and this helps you to keep a close eye on how you are doing;
- complete your reading and note-taking using the techniques described in Chapter 9.

Referencing

The Harvard system of referencing is probably used more than any other. Whenever you refer to a source of material, insert the author's name and the year of publication in brackets. If the author's name is part of the text you just need to insert the year of publication next to it in brackets. If a work is by more than two authors you include only the first, followed by *et al.* You should give full references in alphabetical order at the end of each chapter or at the end of the book.

The format for reports or assignments varies according to the requirements of your organisation but there are some common features. Assignments and projects are very individual but overall yours might look something like this.

Front/Title sheet	Assignment title, your name, personal tutor, etc. (This may be provided by your organisation.)
Abstract	A brief summary of the assignment, probably about a half-page in length.
Table of Contents	List of chapter headings and page numbers, which indicates where the different sections of the assignment can be located.
Introduction/Rationale	Background, purpose and aims.
Methods	Description of how the information was gathered and research procedures that were followed.
Main body	This is where you analyse and discuss all the facts and evidence you have gathered. This is likely to be one of the most substantial sections of the assignment, and may be divided into several sub-sections.
Conclusions	A summary of your findings and the most important points made.
Recommendations	A brief statement on what you feel should be done in the light of your findings.
Appendices	The original information that you have used in compiling the assignment: questionnaires, tables, interviews, etc.
References/Bibliography	A list of published sources you have used, conforming to the Harvard system.

Descriptive, reflective and evaluative writing

There are significant differences between descriptive writing and reflective or evaluative writing. Descriptive writing describes what has happened, as you can see from Val's journal extract.

We worked on punctuation in this morning's session. I went through the different punctuation marks with the whole class and they then took turns punctuating some sentences I wrote on the board. I then gave them a piece to punctuate on their own.

In this extract Val has just described what happened in the session. But reflective writing, such as you should be using in your journal, involves not only thinking about what happened, but why it happened. There are some useful questions to ask yourself to help you write reflectively.

- What went well? Why did it go well?
- What didn't go well? Why didn't it go well?
- What would I do differently next time?

Val's journal extract continues by asking and answering these questions.

The individual punctuation task worked well; they all got down to work and said they had enjoyed doing it. I think the practice on the board really helped to make it work.

We wasted a lot of time at the beginning because no one was keen to come out and do the board punctuations. I think this is because they weren't confident about how to do it. Next time I'm going to spend more time going through the punctuation with the whole class at the beginning so that they know what it's about.

Evaluation is more or less a consequence of reflection. It means to appraise or weigh up something or make a judgement about it. A good question to ask yourself is *how well did this work, how effective or appropriate was it?* All of the journal extracts in this book use reflective and evaluative writing.

Writing for learners

Now is a good time to talk about writing and audience. It isn't that you don't have an audience when you are writing an essay or assignment. You do: the person who will mark your work. If you follow the essay or assignment brief closely you will be writing for that audience. However, most of your writing will be for your learners so they need to be your main focus. We said earlier that writing is purpose-led and the audience, in this case learners, is part of this equation. You need to write in a style that is both appropriate and relevant to them.

PRACTICAL TASK PRACTICAL TASK PRACTICAL TASK PRACTICAL TASK PRACTICAL TASK

Select a group of your learners and make a list of what you know about them. How will this knowledge affect the way you write for them? What do you have to bear in mind when writing for them? Note what you have learnt in your journal.

Preparing handouts, worksheets and PowerPoint presentations

Writing intended for your learners must be of the highest quality. It is unfortunate if you make an error in an assignment but if you make one when you write for learners you give them an erroneous example to follow. And some will follow because they will believe it to be correct. So it is vital that you proof read everything carefully, checking and double-checking.

PRACTICAL TASK PRACTICAL TASK PRACTICAL TASK PRACTICAL TASK PRACTICAL TASK

Why is this a poor handout? List any shortcomings and compare them with the comments below.

How to write handouts

 Avoid using grey or faded handouts.

Use a 12pt or 14 pt font and a clear, non-serif typeface.

You must make sure that you don't let your sentences get too long winded or too complicated with too many-sub clauses, as this can be confusing and annoying for the reader who might get fed up trying to read the words and decide they don't want to carry on.

Make sure the speling is corect.

 Pay attention to layout, using headings and bullet points.

AVOID using Capital Letters except in appropriate contexts.

Some key pointers for selecting or preparing handouts and worksheets have been set out in the companion guide and I have listed them here.

- Avoid using grey or faded handouts.
- Use a 12pt or 14pt font and a clear, non-serif (without feet) typeface such as Arial.
- Use short active sentences: avoid complex sentences with lots of sub-clauses.
- Pay attention to layout, using headings and bullet points.
- When adapting published materials, keep the same layout features as these may aid understanding.
- Use visuals that are relevant to the context to support the text.
- Number pages and lines for clear referencing.
- Avoid using capital letters except in appropriate contexts – the start of a sentence, proper nouns, etc.
- Use key technical terms judiciously and avoid jargon.
- Use clear and unambiguous instructions on worksheets that should be talked through with learners beforehand. Number symbols should also be explained.

These key pointers are even more important when writing for ESOL learners and for learners with specific difficulties or learning disabilities.

Giving written feedback

The question of giving feedback to learners can be contentious. Organisations have vastly different policies on this matter, varying from not allowing teachers to write any comment on learners' work to giving teachers complete freeedom on how they give feedback. So some organisations may require you to leave learners' scripts un-corrected, and others may specify that comment on learners' literacy should be restricted to summative comment. In consequence, your first step is to find out what the policy is in your organisation and to abide by it.

Assuming that you have some discretion, you will find that giving effective written feed-back is an art in itself. The key point is to identify the response you wish to elicit from the learner and to estimate the effect your comments will have. How would you feel if you received the comments in the following task?

PRACTICAL TASK PRACTICAL TASK PRACTICAL TASK PRACTICAL TASK PRACTICAL TASK

Four learners who are in the early part of a GCE A level course in Communication Studies have submitted their essays on the theories of communication. They have just received written feedback on their work from their course tutor. Each of the essays has been graded as a marginal pass.

Read the feedback from the course tutor for these learners. List what you think is wrong with each. Use what you have written to identify the main features of a good feedback report.

Bashir
There are too many grammatical and punctuation errors in this essay. Also, you have not explained Shannon and Weavers model very clearly and some parts of the introduction are difficult to understand.

Catriona
You will need to improve a lot if you want to gain a good A level grade. The essay is too short and there are several areas that you have not covered in enough detail. Look over what you have written carefully and expand those topic areas that are detailed in the briefing sheet which you have not covered in depth.

Joel
You have covered all the main theories and the essay is well structured. Some of your sentences are very long and difficult to understand, and I have marked these in the margins. Please look at these and concentrate on writing shorter, simpler sentences in your next essay. This assignment would have been given a higher grade if

you had included a section on how the theories can be applied to a real life situation, as required in paragraph two of the briefing sheet.

Vivien
This is quite a good essay, but is spoiled by careless spelling and poor presentation.

The feedback for Bashir and Catriona is negative, with no attempt made to identify the strengths of the essay. In the case of Bashir, it is unwise to criticise a learner's punctuation while making a mistake of your own in the comment (which, of course, you spotted straight away).

Of the four feedback reports, Joel's is clearly the most effective. The writer has identified the strengths of the essay and has given constructive feedback to help the learner to improve. Furthermore, the use of marginal comments will enable the learner to identify precisely where the errors have occurred.

The feedback for Vivien does give some credit to the learner but the comments are so generalised that they are almost meaningless. It will be well nigh impossible for Vivien and also Catriona, to work out where they have gone wrong and how to put it right.

Here are some guidelines for effective written feedback.

- Identify the strengths of the assignment and give this some prominence in the report.
- Be specific in identifying where and what shortcomings exist, using marginal comments where appropriate. Simple error analysis, where a code is used in margins to mark errors, encourages learners to work independently to correct mistakes (see next chapter).
- State clearly what the learner needs to do to improve.
- Separate feedback on content from that on language use.

Supporting learners

Adult learners often begin a programme of learning following a number of years away from education. For some, this may be their first experience of contributing to discussions and of academic writing since they finished formal education. Because a learning environment is a familiar one to us we don't always appreciate how daunting it can be for others. Learners often put on a brave face and muddle along and most of them do get used to talking in front of others.

Writing is a different matter. Writing an essay or an assignment will probably be the first time in a learning programme that a learner will have to perform. Many will feel that they are indeed *on show* even if it is only you, the teacher, who will be looking. This can be terrifying and, rather than face failure, some will drift away. Even for those who do take the plunge, it can still be an uncomfortable experience. Almost all learners discover that with some practice they can write. This success is often accompanied by the realisation that their problem was one of a lack of confidence rather than lack of writing skills.

We can help learners to develop their writing skills as they learn about their specialist subject. We can integrate writing into their subject learning when we use strategies that engage them in the process of writing. When this is done skilfully learners gain confidence along with their writing skills. So how does it work?

Let's illustrate this by having a look at Jude, a lecturer in the catering department of his local college, who is studying for QTLS. He is writing in his reflective journal about his experience of trying out an idea he had for integrating writing into an NVQ level 2 programme in food preparation and cooking.

SCENARIO STUDY – JUDE'S JOURNAL

We'd been discussing ways to include literacy, numeracy and ICT in our teaching sessions and I had this idea about getting my learners to write a booklet on hygiene when handling food. This group has only been with me a couple of weeks so I don't know them too well but I know from the initial assessment that they cover a range of ability.

The first thing that took me by surprise was how time consuming it is. For a start I had to design a guide that was detailed enough to support those who needed some extra help, but not too detailed so that they were just filling in boxes. This took me a while. Then I had to find some models of similar booklets to get them started. But it wasn't just my time; I discovered that it takes up their time as well and time is something we are short of on this programme. To be honest, they have to know this stuff to get their qualification; it would be much easier and quicker if we just did it in class, but I wanted to give this a go.

The second problem was their reaction when I introduced the idea at the next session. Naively, I thought they'd jump at it but they didn't even move. Stunned I think, but I persevered and we had a reasonable class discussion on what they wanted their booklet to achieve and who they were writing it for – most decided it would be useful in their workplace.

We discussed the model booklets and then I got them into small groups and let them get on with it. They already had their textbooks which had all the information they needed. Each group was producing its own booklet. I had told them that they should decide how to divide up the work but that they were each responsible for contributing a certain number of words to the booklet.

I knew that some would need extra help so I worked my way around the class and managed to talk to everyone before the end of the session. By the time we finished everyone had a first draft of the piece they were writing so I felt quite pleased. I told them to make sure that they read their work carefully and also to try to get someone else to read it to make sure it made sense and to check for spelling and punctuation. It had to be ready by the next session because we only had a limited amount of time to get everything on to the computer and to put in some illustrations.

Well, the booklets came out OK and the learners were very pleased with them and with themselves - they had actually gained enthusiasm as we went along. But I can't say that the booklets were good. They had all included the relevant information, so that was good, and they certainly learnt about hygiene, probably better than if we had done it in class, so that was good too. But the writing wasn't great and some of the fonts they had chosen were totally inappropriate. There were quite a few errors too. I was really annoyed with myself because it was my fault. I realise that I shouldn't have just relied on them to proof read; I think some of them didn't bother. Somehow I'd forgotten that this was the whole point – to improve their writing skills. We should have had a session on proof reading in class – I could have fixed up some examples of common mistakes. It might even have been better if they had worked in pairs. They each have their strong points and could have helped each other. I'll certainly try that next time.

PRACTICAL TASK PRACTICAL TASK PRACTICAL TASK PRACTICAL TASK PRACTICAL TASK

Was Jude's approach to incorporating writing into his lesson appropriate? What comments would you make to him after reading about his experience?

Jude needs to be applauded for putting into practice his idea on incorporating writing into his teaching session on hygiene and for all the extra work he put in. It seems to have worked well. Although initially reluctant, the learners gained enthusiasm and were proud of what they had done. They also appeared to have learned some important points better than if Jude had used his usual teaching strategy. Jude was pretty hard on himself. Yes, a session on proof reading would have been very useful and paired working was also a good idea, but he will include them next time

Jude's experience shows that there are strategies we can use to develop learners' writing within the context of their subject area.

- Use writing models. Give an example of a how a booklet, assignment or essay might look. This will help trigger ideas that learners can then develop.
- Use writing frames if appropriate. These are templates that provide a scaffold for specific writing tasks, and vary with the task to be done. The essay format in this chapter is an example of a writing frame, and you can design a frame for your own purposes.
- Drafting and proof reading are important and need to be included in the writing process.
- Working in pairs, group work and discussion will support learners in their writing activities.
- Learners need guidance on appropriate fonts and layout when using ICT to produce work.

A SUMMARY OF KEY POINTS

> Writing has a formal structure involving sentences and paragraphs.

> Purpose and audience will influence the style and format of a piece of writing.

> To be effective, writing should be clear, concise, correct, coherent, consistent and complete.

> Your writing for learners should be error-free, appropriate and relevant to their needs.

> Your feedback to learners should identify the strengths of their writing, be specific on errors and use strategies that encourage them to work independently to improve their writing.

> Writing models and frames, drafting and proof reading activities will help learners to develop their writing skills.

Branching options

The following tasks are designed to help you consolidate and develop your writing skills and those of your learners.

Reflection

How do you assess the writing skills of your learners and what feedback do you give them on their writing? Consider whether it is appropriate and sufficient.

Analysis

Select and analyse a piece of your writing in relation to the six criteria for effective writing detailed in this chapter. You may find it useful to use one of your written assignments for this purpose. Is it clear, concise, correct, consistent, coherent and complete? Identify any areas where you could improve the quality of your writing and note these in your journal.

Research

Writers use a variety of devices to make their writing more interesting and to gain the effects they desire. Many of these devices can be grouped under the heading of figures of speech, and they all have their strengths. They have weaknesses as well. For example, similes can become clichéd and lose their force, for example, *sick as a parrot*, and metaphors can be mixed, e.g. *burning the midnight oil at both ends*. Use your library or the internet to find out more about the following figures of speech and try to identify their strengths and weaknesses in the context of your professional role:

Alliteration	Euphemism	Hyperbole
Irony	Litotes	Metaphor
Oxymoron	Personification	Synecdoche

REFERENCES AND FURTHER READING REFERENCES AND FURTHER READING

Fairbairn, J and Winch, C (1993) *Reading, writing and reasoning; a guide for students.* Maidenhead: Open University Press.

Finnegan, R (1975) Unit 8: Communication and technology, in Open University (ed) *Communication*. Buckingham: Open University Press.

LLUK (November 2007) *Inclusive learning approaches for literacy, language, numeracy and ICT.* London: LLUK (the companion guide).

Palmer, R (1993) *Write in style: a guide to good English*. London: Chapman and Hall.

Petit, P (2002) *To reach the clouds*. New York: North Point Press.

11
Grammar, punctuation and spelling

This chapter will help you to:

- understand some of the rules and conventions of grammar, punctuation and spelling;
- explore ways of developing your own skills in grammar, punctuation and spelling and those of your learners.

Links to minimum core elements:
A 2.8   Communicating the written process.
A 2.10   Developing spelling and punctuation skills.
B 9   Write fluently, accurately and legibly on a range of topics.
B 11   Use spelling and punctuation accurately in order to make meaning clear.
B 12   Understand and use the conventions of grammar (the forms and structures of words, phrases, clauses, sentences and texts) consistently when producing written text.

Links to LLUK Professional Standards for QTLS:
AS4, AS7, AK5.1, BK3.1, BK3.3, BK3.4, BP3.1, BP3.3, BP3.4, CK3.4, CP3.4.

Links to LLUK mandatory units of assessment:
Planning and enabling learning (CTLLS and DTLLS):
- understand how to use a range of communication skills and methods to communicate effectively with learners and relevant parties in own organisation;
- understand and demonstrate knowledge of the minimum core in own practice.

Enabling learning and assessment (DTLLS):
- understand and demonstrate how to give effective feedback to promote learner progress and achievement;
- understand and demonstrate knowledge of the minimum core in own practice.

Theories and principles for planning and enabling learning (DTLLS):
- understand and demonstrate knowledge of the minimum core in own practice.

Introduction

Few people can look at a chapter entitled grammar, punctuation and spelling and feel excited at the prospect of reading it. Yet the rules and conventions that serve and support the English language reflect just how dynamic our language is. Indeed, throughout its history English has constantly mutated as new words are introduced or old ones change their meaning. William Shakespeare, for example, created new words whenever he felt like it. In fact, he introduced over 300 new words just by adding the suffix *un-*, for example, *unmask, unhand, unlock* (Bryson, 2007).

As society changes, our language changes to accommodate it. Consider how English has been enriched by absorbing words such as *bungalow, jubilee, coffee* and *gymkhana*. Changes in technology have also led to the introduction of new words and phrases: *aircraft, cinema, package tour, hard drive* and *broadband* are just a few of the numerous examples.

Language rules and conventions have to accommodate the diverse nature of English if we are to interpret its meaning accurately. It is vital for us as teachers to have a good understanding of these rules so that we can act as role models for learners. In this chapter we examine the rules of grammar, punctuation and spelling, consider ways to develop your skills and look how you can help learners to develop their skills.

Grammar

The following is a summary of grammatical rules, with a limited number of examples for each point. Depending on how confident you feel about grammar, you could work through it or use it as a reference, dipping in to fill in any gaps in your knowledge. In any event don't get too bogged down in names and definitions. You can find out more about grammar and writing in general in *Write in style*, by Richard Palmer. It gives lots of examples and tasks and is very readable.

> *Language – including and especially everyday usage – does not serve grammar: it is the other way round.*
>
> (Palmer, 1993, p231)

We can define grammar as rules and conventions that govern the relationships between words. This grammar section covers:

- words, and the eight parts of speech;
- sentences;
- common errors in writing sentences.

Words and the eight parts of speech

The usual starting point for a study of grammar is to consider words and their uses. Bear in mind, however, that words themselves can be analysed in linguistic terms. The smallest unit of sound is a phoneme, and there are about 44 of these in English. Examples of phonemes are *buy, high, cry*. A grapheme is the written representation of a phoneme. The next stage is a morpheme, which is the smallest language unit that makes sense. Some morphemes make sense on their own, for example, *bend*, while some need to be linked to others, for example, prefixes and suffixes like *un-* and *-ing*. A word can comprise one or more morphemes, for example, *unbending*.

In writing, words are used in different ways, related to their different jobs within sentences. We can divide words more or less into eight groups depending on the job they do in conveying the meaning of a sentence:

Noun:	is used to name something
Pronoun:	stands in for a noun

Verb:	denotes a state or action
Adverb:	gives information about a verb or another adverb
Adjective:	describes a noun
Preposition:	indicates time or place
Conjunction:	joins parts of a sentence
Interjection:	expresses mood or reaction

When we divide words into different groups, as we have here, it looks as though a word always acts as the same part of speech, but this isn't so. Words can, and do, act as a number of different parts of speech depending on the situation and context. For example, *travel* can be used as a noun (*travel is wonderful*), a verb (*we travel frequently*), or an adjective (*travel sickness*).

Nouns

Nouns are the names of things, people, places, thoughts or feelings. There are four types of nouns, common nouns, proper nouns, abstract nouns and collective nouns.

Common nouns name:

objects:	*table, handout, car*
places:	*town, street, college*
living creatures:	*frog, learner, women*

Proper nouns require capital initial letters and are the actual names of:

people:	*Rafael, George, Miriam*
places:	*Germany, High Street, The Cotswolds*
organisations:	*McDonald's, Nike, Greenpeace*

Abstract nouns name:

feelings:	*sadness, fear, joy*
ideas:	*freedom, democracy*
qualities:	*honesty, bravery*

Collective nouns name a group:

a *bunch* of roses
a *fleet* of ships
a *school* of porpoises

In some languages, such as French, all nouns are either masculine or feminine, even if they are the names of objects, places or feelings. In English we assign gender only to living creatures (the exception being ships and aircraft, which are customarily referred to as *she*). We use the pronoun or adjective to indicate the gender, for example, ***he*** *is the man who always washes **his** car on Sunday.*

Adjectives

Adjectives describe nouns, for example: *large, green, wet, beautiful.*

There are several sub-groups of adjectives that you may come across, for example:

- possessive adjectives: ***my*** book, ***their*** house, ***its*** taste, ***our*** problem
- demonstrative adjectives: ***the*** girl (the definite article), ***a*** girl, ***some*** girls (the indefinite article), ***this*** table, ***those*** computers
- interrogative adjectives: ***What*** car? ***Which*** teacher?

Pronouns

Pronouns replace nouns, for example: *Laura went shopping and Laura bought a dress* becomes, *Laura went shopping and **she** bought a dress.*

Like adjectives, pronouns can be sub-divided into specific groups, for example:

- possessive pronouns: ***mine**, **yours***
- demonstrative pronouns: ***these**, **those***
- interrogative pronouns: ***What**? **Who**?*

Verbs

Verbs are action words; they tell you what is happening: *finish, laugh, walk,* or about existing or feeling: *am, was, believe.* For example:

> She *finished* her work.
> They *are* all here.
> I *believe* it will rain tomorrow.

The simplest form of a verb is called the infinitive. You can recognise it because it has a *to* in front of it, for example, *to be, to run,* or *to eat.* You would say, *I want **to eat** my lunch* or *he would like **to believe** what she said.* More often, though, we use verbs in their finite form, for example, *the child **ran** away* and *she **walks** her dog,* from the infinitives *to run* and *to walk.*

Verbs establish when something takes place: in the present, the future or the past.

Present tense:	*I work*
	I am working
Future tense:	*I shall work*
	I shall be working
	I am going to work
Past tense:	*I worked* (called the preterite or past historic tense)
	I have worked (the perfect tense)
	I was working (the imperfect tense)

(Note: There is a whole series of past tenses; each one conveys a slightly different meaning.)

Some verb forms can be used to form compound tenses, or as nouns or adjectives. These are called participles. There are two kinds of participle: the past participle, which usually ends in *d* or *ed,* for example, *reasoned, painted, decided,* and the present participle which ends in *ing,* for example, *reasoning, painting, deciding.* For instance, you would say, *I have **baked** a cake* (past participle creating a compound tense), and ***baking** is messy* (present participle used as a noun).

Verbs used to command or entreat are known as imperatives, for example, *Stop! Let's go!*

Adverbs

Just as adjectives describe nouns, adverbs describe/modify verbs, or how something is done, for example, *easily, quickly, carefully, often, accidentally.*

Prepositions

Prepositions indicate position or place, for example, *in, behind, below, among*, or time, *before, until, since.*

Conjunctions

Conjunctions are joining words. They indicate relationships, for example, *and, because, so*, or differences, for example, *but, whereas, although.*

Interjections

Interjections express emotions such as surprise, doubt or excitement, for example, *Well! Hey! Never! Ah! Help!*

Sentences

Sentences give our writing a formal structure but they can be slippery to define. One definition, *a sentence begins with a capital letter and ends in a full stop*, sounds good. However, you could use a capital letter and a full stop with any old group of words but it wouldn't necessarily mean they formed a sentence. Here are two more definitions.

A sentence will express a complete thought

She baked a cake for tea. This is straightforward enough. Here is a complete thought. Let's try breaking the sentence into two bits.

She baked. This is still a sentence because it expresses a complete thought.

a cake for tea This isn't a sentence because it doesn't express a complete thought. It leaves you thinking, *well, what about this cake for tea?* This group of words is in fact a phrase, which is defined as a group of two or more words that do not make sense on their own but form part of a sentence.

A sentence must contain a subject and a verb

Just to remind ourselves, a verb is a word that says what is happening (often called a doing word) or is about existing or feeling. The subject of a sentence is who or what is doing or existing or feeling. If this sounds tricky, look at these examples.

She walks to work.
The wind howled.
I am at home tomorrow.
We believe it will rain soon.

Walks, howled, am and *believe* are the verbs. *She, the wind, I* and *we* are the subjects.

If a group of words has a subject and a verb then you have a clause. If, additionally, this clause makes complete sense, then you have a sentence. The first eleven words of this paragraph, *If a group of words has a subject and a verb* is a clause but not a sentence, as it does not make sense on its own.

So, in summary, to recognise whether or not a group of words makes a sentence there are two conditions to be fulfilled. Does it express a complete thought? Does it contain a subject and a verb?

Sentences can also have an object as well as a subject and a verb. In the sentence *She baked a cake*, the cake is the object and the rest of the sentence tells us what is being done to it.

So far we have looked at simple sentences that express one thought. Lots of sentences are compound, with two or more sentences linked by conjunctions, *She baked a cake for tea but it wasn't eaten.* Similarly, complex sentences can contain several clauses as long as one of them makes complete sense (the main clause). The other clauses are called subordinate clauses. One of the sentences in the introduction to this chapter is structured like this. *As society changes, our language changes to accommodate it,* is made up of a main clause, *our language changes to accommodate it,* and one subordinate clause, *As our society changes.*

Constructing sentences is a skill that develops with practice but here are some thoughts that are worth bearing in mind.

Make sure you know what you want to say before you begin your sentence

This might seem obvious but we don't always bother to do it. So, before you begin writing, think about what you want your sentence to say. Try to imagine how it will actually sound when you read it.

Trust your own judgement

When you read your work back, do it carefully and honestly; you will usually have a feel for whether it sounds right or not. If it sounds right, good, trust your judgement. If it doesn't sound right, you may not know what is wrong but the rule still applies. Trust your judgement; if it sounds wrong it probably is. The best thing to do if this happens is to step away. Go for a walk or sleep on it. Alternatively, you could ask a friend to read it and give you feedback.

Try to make your sentences more active than passive

In an active sentence the subject acts: *The dog chewed the bone.* In a passive sentence the subject is acted upon: *The bone was chewed by the dog.* Active writing is more straightforward although there are times when passive writing is more appropriate, for example, when you want to soften the effect of your message, *Your attendance is required at court on …* rather than, *Attend court on …*

Some grammar rules can be broken

Here are three rules we don't have to follow.

- Don't begin a sentence with *and* or *but*. You can, but don't do it too often.
- Don't use the apostrophe to shorten words. You can. It's not always necessary to write *it is* or *do not* or *you are* in full; you can write *it's*, or *don't* or *you're*. There may be times when you feel it is appropriate to write words in full but don't become too hung up on it. There is more about apostrophes in the punctuation section of this chapter.
- Never end a sentence with a preposition. You can. In fact sometimes you need to or the sentence becomes so clumsy it sounds ridiculous. There is an anecdote in Sir Ernest Gower's *The Complete Plain Words* (1954) concerning Winston Churchill. An editor had clumsily rearranged one of Churchill's sentences to avoid ending it in a preposition and the Prime Minister, very proud of his style, scribbled this note in reply: *This is the sort of English up with which I will not put!*

Common errors in writing sentences

We saw in the previous chapter that the rules and conventions of grammar are in place to help us understand the meaning of the text. Even though, as we've just seen, some rules can be ignored, most do need to be followed. In the following task a number of grammatical rules and conventions have been broken.

PRACTICAL TASK PRACTICAL TASK PRACTICAL TASK PRACTICAL TASK PRACTICAL TASK

Read the following sentences. Each one has a common grammatical error. Identify the error and write each sentence correctly.

1 This present is from David and I.
2 An extensive range of lipsticks are on offer today.
3 When a masseur becomes qualified they can open a salon.
4 He doesn't want nothing to eat.
5 There are less people here today than yesterday.
6 When the dog trod on the mouse it fled in terror.
7 Writing the introduction last, making sure it covers all the points in the essay.
8 He was the happiest of the two brothers.

Here are the corrected sentences.

1 This present is from David and *me*.
   An easy way to remember whether to use *I* or *me* is to say the sentence without the other person, in this case, *this present is from me*. It doesn't make sense to say, *this present is from I*. On the other hand, *David and I are buying a present* becomes, *I am buying a present* so it is correct to use *I* rather than *me*.
2 An extensive range of lipsticks *is* on offer today.
   The subject *range* is singular so the verb *is* must agree.
3 When a masseur becomes qualified *he* can open a salon.
   The subject *masseur* is masculine so the pronoun *he* must agree. It is, however, becoming more acceptable to use *they* in place of *he/she* when the subject could be masculine or feminine.
4 He doesn't want *anything* to eat.
   This error is known as a double negative and literally means that if he doesn't want nothing he actually wants something!
5 There are *fewer* people here today than yesterday.
   Use *fewer* with objects that can be counted one-by-one. Use *less* with qualities or quantities that cannot be individually counted.
6 *The mouse fled in terror when the dog trod on it*.
   The sentence is not clear about who fled, the mouse or the dog. Re-arrange it so that the subject is next to the verb.
7 *I am writing the introduction last, making sure it covers all the points in the essay*.
   This is an incomplete sentence which needs a subject.
8 He was the *happier* of the two brothers.
   It would need more than two brothers for him to be the happiest.

Happy   Happier   Happiest

Punctuation

We use punctuation in our writing to help convey our intended meaning and alterations in punctuation can alter this meaning. Look at these two letters.

> *Dear Jack,*
> *I want a man who knows what love is all about. You are generous, kind, thoughtful. People who are not like you admit to being useless and inferior. You have ruined me for other men. I yearn for you. I have no feelings whatsoever when we're apart. I can be forever happy – will you let me be yours?*
> *Jill*

And

> *Dear Jack,*
> *I want a man who knows what love is. All about you are generous, kind, thoughtful people, who are not like you. Admit to being useless and inferior. You have ruined me. For other men I yearn! For you I have no feelings whatsoever. When we're apart I can be forever happy. Will you let me be?*
> *Yours,*
> *Jill*

(Truss, 2003, pp9–10)

As you see, the words in each passage are identical but the meaning of each is quite different. Clearly then, punctuation has a very important job. Let's look at some of the punctuation devices we have at hand to give our writing clarity, meaning and emphasis. We have:

- commas;
- full stops, question marks and exclamation marks;
- semi-colons;
- colons;
- dashes/hyphens;
- brackets;
- apostrophes.

Commas

Commas are straightforward enough. We use them in the following ways.

- A comma indicates a pause between two parts of the sentence, making the meaning of the sentence clearer: *Because of the accident, I was late getting to work.*

- A comma separates a word or phrase in a sentence that doesn't have to be included. Here you would use a comma on either side of the word or phrase: *My mother, who is very fit, walks to work every day. I have, in my house, many paintings*.
- A comma breaks up a list of *items: I have two dogs, one cat, a goldfish, a stick insect and a hamster*.

Full stops, question marks and exclamation marks

These don't usually cause us problems either. We use them in the following ways.

- A full stop indicates the end of a sentence: *Please come in*.
- A full stop indicates an abbreviation: U.K., Lincs., Prof., Maj., a.m., no., etc. In recent usage there has been a tendency to omit full stops in this context. For example, they are now rarely used in addresses.
- We use a question mark when a direct question is asked: *Where are you going*? But it is not used when an indirect question is asked: *He asked me where I was going*.
- We use an exclamation mark to show excitement, anger, surprise or humour: *Be quiet! Don't! Well! Ho!* Be sparing in your use of exclamation marks or they lose their value.

Semi-colons

Semi-colons can be a little tricky. We use them in the following ways.

- They can replace conjunctions when comparing two things: *This morning it rained; this afternoon it's sunny*, in place of: *This morning it rained but this afternoon it's sunny*.
- They can replace full stops where two statements are closely linked: *Please be seated; we are about to begin*, in place of: *Please be seated. We are about to begin*.

Colons

These, too, can sometimes be tricky. We use colons in the following ways.

- They introduce a list: *You will need the following things: pencil, paper, compass and stopwatch*.
- They indicate a big contrast between two statements in a sentence: *I wanted her to have a big wedding: instead she decided to elope!*

Dashes/hyphens

Dashes/hyphens have a number of uses. We use them in the following ways.

- To emphasise: *He's a star – the tops*.
- To separate phrases when writing informally: *See you tomorrow – not sure what time*.
- To link words: *Up-date*.

Brackets

Brackets shouldn't pose any problem. We use them to indicate that a statement is separate from the rest of the sentence. *I paid 100 euros (£90.00) to hire the car for a week.* When the brackets are at the end of the sentence you need to be careful where you place the full stop. Normally it goes outside the brackets. *He bought me a necklace (the one I'd always wanted).* However, if the statement within the brackets is a complete sentence you place the full stop inside the brackets. *He bought me a necklace. (It was the one I'd always wanted.)*

Apostrophes

Of all punctuation, it's the apostrophe that gives us the most anguish. Knowing what to do with it is almost like being a member of an exclusive club. You're either in or you're out. If you're in, you can snigger at apostrophe errors. If you're out, you live in apostrophic (my word) fear. So maligned and abused is the apostrophe, it has its own protection society. In 2001 John Richards, a former journalist and sub-editor, fed up with seeing the apostrophe so ill-treated, set up The Apostrophe Protection Society, (www.apostrophe.fsnet.co.uk) in an attempt to save, what he calls, the threatened species.

Apostrophe rules are not difficult and there are not many to remember.

- You use an apostrophe with a noun to show that something belongs. If the noun is singular you add **s** and place the apostrophe in front of it.

The girl's crayons.	Crayons which belong to one girl.
The lady's hat.	A hat which belongs to one lady.
My sister's cars	Cars which belong to one sister.

If the noun is plural you place the apostrophe after the **s**.

The girls' crayons	Crayons which belong to more than one girl.
The ladies' hats	Hats which belong to more than one lady.
My sisters' cars	Cars which belong to more than one sister.

- Some nouns, for example, *child* and *man*, don't have an s to show they are plural: instead, they change their form to *children* and *men*. To indicate that something belongs to these nouns you add an **s** and place the apostrophe in front of it, *the children's shoes, the men's coats*.
- You use an apostrophe when you shorten a word to show that a letter has been omitted.

you are	*you're*	we will	*we'll*
let us	*let's*	do not	*don't*
it is	*it's*	it is not	*it isn't*

The only thing you have to look out for is not to get confused between you're and your or between it's and its. *You're* indicates that you have shortened the words *you are*: **You're** *looking well this morning. Your* indicates that something belongs: *Here is* **your** *book. It's* indicates that you have shortened it *is*: **It's** *cold today. Its* indicates that something belongs: *Look at that tree;* **its** *leaves are golden.* (Note: although *its* here is a possesive adjective there is no apostrophe, just like in the possessive pronouns *hers, yours, ours, theirs*. None of them has an apostrophe.)

Dialogue

Recording the actual words people use is reasonably straightforward. Have a look at this example.

'You're late again!' *said Joseph.* **'Where have you been?'**
'I forgot my assignment,' *Kerry sighed,* **'and had to go back for it.'**
Joseph decided to hide his irritation, and contented himself with saying, **'Well you're here now. Come and sit down.'**

There are two parts to a piece of writing that contains dialogue: direct speech (the words actually spoken) and the narrative (the words describing the story). Here are the main punctuation rules.

- The dialogue (written in bold above to illustrate the point) is enclosed in inverted commas.

- The punctuation of the dialogue is put inside the inverted commas.
- You need a new paragraph for each new speaker.
- If the dialogue is interrupted by the narrative, commas are used to signpost the change from direct speech to narrative and vice-versa. (See Kerry's statement on the second line.)

PRACTICAL TASK PRACTICAL TASK PRACTICAL TASK PRACTICAL TASK PRACTICAL TASK

To illustrate how punctuation can affect meaning, work out how many ways the following sentences can be punctuated.

1   john said martha likes to cook the boys meals

2   well come tomorrow susan said at lunchtime

There are quite a number of possibilities. I can think of about half a dozen for each one.

John said Martha likes to cook the boy's meals.
John said Martha likes to cook the boys' meals.
John said, 'Martha likes to cook the boy's meals.'
John said, 'Martha likes to cook the boys' meals.'
'John,' said Martha, 'likes to cook the boys' meals.'
'John,' said Martha, 'likes to cook the boy's meals.'

'Well, come tomorrow,' Susan said at lunchtime.
'Well, come tomorrow,' Susan said, 'at lunchtime.'
'We'll come tomorrow,' Susan said at lunchtime.
'We'll come tomorrow,' Susan said, 'at lunchtime.'
'Well, come tomorrow,' Susan said, 'at lunchtime?'
'We'll come tomorrow,' Susan said. 'At lunchtime?'

For a lively, entertaining and informative book on punctuation, read *Eats, Shoots and Leaves*, by Lynn Truss (2003).

Spelling

Beware of heard, a dreadful word,
That looks like beard and sounds like bird,
And dead: it's said like bed, not bead,
For goodness' sake, don't call it deed!
Watch out for meat and great and threat;
They rhyme with suite and straight and debt.
                                                    Anon

English has had such a chequered history it is hardly surprising that we have few spelling rules based on common sense. The Romans, Vikings and Anglo-Saxons have all had a hand in the formation of the English language. According to Wakelin (1988), after the Norman conquest, Anglo-Norman, an English dialect of French, became the official language, although English still continued to be written. When English was re-established in the fourteenth century it was very different to its pre-Norman form. Writers such as Geoffrey Chaucer and William Tyndale attempted to give spelling a consistent system but educated people still wrote in French and Latin.

When printing was introduced in the fifteenth century books were often printed with words spelt at the whim of the printer. English spelling during this long period was so arbitrary that a dictionary published in 1604, *A table alphabeticall of hard words,* spelled *words* two different ways on the title page (Bryson, 2007*)*. It wasn't until Samuel Johnson produced his dictionary in 1755 that any real system appeared; it was a system that set in concrete all the oddities and idiosyncrasies that are now accepted as correct spelling. We have to live with the consequences of this haphazard development; it's easy to appreciate why we are so often tripped up.

One feature of contemporary English is the number of letter patterns that are pronounced in many different ways. A good example of this is *ough*, and the contrasting pronunciations of *bough, cough, thought, through* and *tough*. Conversely, many graphemes (sounds expressed in writing) are spelt in a variety of ways. So the *s* sound in *ways* is spelt with *sc* in *science,* with *c* in *ceiling*, and even with *psy* in *psychology*. English also contains many homophones, words that sound the same but have different meanings or spellings; *site, sight* and *cite* are examples. All this means that spelling can be inconsistent and complicated. This often causes problems for learners. It can be particularly difficult for those whose mother tongue is one where the spelling consistently matches the phonemes of the language, such as German or Spanish.

PRACTICAL TASK PRACTICAL TASK PRACTICAL TASK PRACTICAL TASK PRACTICAL TASK

Some words are especially confusing. Look at the following word pairs, and identify the difference between each word in the pair. Check your response by reference to the internet or a grammar book.

Accept	Except
Affect	Effect
Aural	Oral
Comprehensible	Comprehensive
Council	Counsel
Currant	Current
Dependant	Dependent
Desert	Dessert
Elicit	Illicit
Formally	Formerly
Ingenious	Ingenuous
Lose	Loose
Moral	Morale
Principal	Principle
Stationary	Stationery

PRACTICAL TASK PRACTICAL TASK PRACTICAL TASK PRACTICAL TASK PRACTICAL TASK

A number of these words are incorrectly spelt. See if you can identify them and write down the correct spelling. Then check your answers with the aid of a dictionary.

accommodation	liason	rythm	embarassment
necessary	arguement	innoculate	business
twelth	discrete	concensus	drunkeness
harrasment	independant	fourty	mischevious
relavent	desparate	suceed	changeable

Some spelling rules and strategies

Because of its chequered history we know that, unlike grammar and punctuation, spelling doesn't consistently follow a set of rules. True, there are spelling rules but they often have so many exceptions that it sometimes hardly seems worth the effort. Nevertheless, there are a few that are quite helpful and easy to remember.

- *i* before *e* except after *c* – but only when the sound is *ee*. For example, *believe*, *relieve*, *series*, *achieve*, *hygiene* and *receive*, *deceive*, *conceive*, *ceiling*, but *neigh*, *veil*, *reign*, *eight*, *their*.
- For nouns ending in *y* change the *y* to an *i* and add *es* to make them plural. For example, *try – tries; lady – ladies; hobby – hobbies*.
- To add *ing* to a verb, use a double consonant for short vowel verbs but a single consonant for long vowel verbs. Short vowel verbs: *tap – tapping, sit – sitting, let – letting, knit – knitting, run – running*. Long vowel verbs: *wait – waiting, hope – hoping, deal – dealing*.
- The silent *e*. Adding an *e* at the end of a word changes the sound of the vowel from its short to its long form: *pin* to *pine*, *rat* to *rate*, *win* to *wine*.

Very few people are completely confident in spelling and the ability to misspell words is no respecter of persons. US Vice President Dan Quayle found this out the hard way in 1992 when he was asking students to write words on the board. Twelve-year-old William Figueroa wrote *potato*, but Quayle told him to add an *e*, much to the delight of media critics. Most of us have our stumbling blocks even if they come in various sizes: if yours is large you can make it smaller. My own stumbling block used to be huge, as you can see from the extract from one of my school reports in Figure 11.1. Now it is smaller; it shrank significantly during a period when I worked in an office typing letters from short-hand notes. Any letter with a spelling error was returned to me for re-typing!

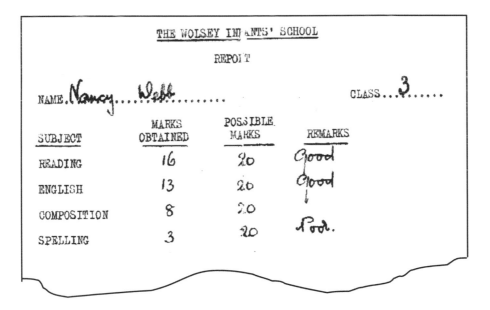

Figure 11.1 Must try harder!

There are some useful strategies for cutting stumbling blocks down to size. You can use them to develop your spelling skills: you can also suggest, when appropriate, that learners make use of them.

- Don't be lazy with spelling.
- Use mnemonics.
- Keep a dictionary handy.
- Read with care.
- Look, cover, write, check.
- Create icons from troublesome letters.

Don't be lazy with spelling

Imagine that, like me, if you misspell words you'll have to type your work out again. I guarantee that this focuses your mind and compels you to check and double-check everything you write.

Use mnemonics

A mnemonic is a device that helps you to remember, for example, *spring forward/ fall back* is a mnemonic to remember to put clocks forward in spring but back in autumn (fall). The best mnemonics to use are the ones you make up yourself. Here are a few examples to get you started.

Principal	The princi*pal* is my *pal*.
Hear (not here)	You h*ear* with your *ear*.
Because	*B*etty *e*ats *c*ake *a*nd *u*ses *s*even *e*ggs.

PRACTICAL TASK PRACTICAL TASK PRACTICAL TASK PRACTICAL TASK PRACTICAL TASK

Make up a mnemonic for each of these words: arbitrary, embarrass, facetious, liaison, manoeuvre.

Keep a dictionary handy

Get into the habit of looking up words that you struggle with. After a while you'll find that you only need to check that you have spelt them correctly; soon you won't need to look them up at all. Spell-check is also useful; it isn't infallible but it will pick up most of your errors.

Read with care

Spelling is a visual skill. Be more observant when you read. Take time to look and recognise the syllables and the word patterns; it can sometimes help to run your finger along the line as you read. Word games such as Scrabble, crossword puzzles and anagrams are also useful.

Look, cover, write, check

This is a tried and tested strategy for improving spelling. *Look* carefully at the word and focus on the bit that is giving you problems. *Cover* the word. *Write* it from memory. *Check* back and if you don't get it right first time, keep going until you do.

Create icons from troublesome letters

For words that you find particularly difficult, turn the troublesome letters into meaningful icons, as in Figure 11.2.

Figure 11.2 Icons attract attention

PRACTICAL TASK PRACTICAL TASK PRACTICAL TASK PRACTICAL TASK PRACTICAL TASK

Create icons for these words: questionnaire, business, rhythm.

For a more in-depth look at spelling I suggest you read *Getting to grips with spelling* by Catherine Hilton and Margaret Hyde (1992).

Supporting learners

We said in earlier chapters that, as teachers, we should be providing a model for our learners. In this respect grammar, punctuation and spelling are no different from, say, speaking and listening. If we give learners the impression that these skills aren't important to us, there is no reason for them to take a different viewpoint. On the other hand, if our board work and handouts are error-free we show learners that we value good English.

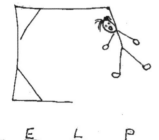

Time is always in short supply in teaching and I'm sure your teaching programmes are no exception. In the long run, however, dedicating time within a programme to dealing with grammar, punctuation and spelling problems when they arise does help learners to progress in their subject area. You can focus on specific areas or ask learners where they feel they need help. Word games are also good, especially for spelling difficult or technical words and are fun: try hangman.

PRACTICAL TASK PRACTICAL TASK PRACTICAL TASK PRACTICAL TASK PRACTICAL TASK

Make a list of the technical words from your subject area that might be difficult for some learners to spell. Consider strategies for helping learners spell them correctly.

You may feel that it would be appropriate to encourage particular learners to use some of the spelling strategies mentioned earlier. You do need to be sensitive in your approach. It is most important that you talk to each learner, find out what they would like and suggest strategies only if you feel confident that the learner would be enthusiastic, for example, if they ask you for ideas to improve their spelling.

Error analysis marking encourages learners to develop self-correcting skills. When you mark learners' work, instead of correcting the errors, place a mark in the margin to indicate that there is an error in that line. It is best to use a code, but make sure the learners understand it first. Some examples might be *S* for spelling, *P* for punctuation, *SS* for sentence structure, or *V* for vocabulary.

You can use error analysis marking in a way that suits your learners. For example you can:

- put a code in the margin and underline the error in the line;
- put a code in the margin but allow the learner find the error in that line;
- put a note at the bottom of the text, for example, *find five spelling errors*;
- encourage learners to do error analysis of each other's writing;
- encourage learners to do their own proof reading;
- indicate only major errors.

Remember that you need to be aware of, and follow, your organisation's policy on marking learners' work before you undertake any error analysis marking.

A SUMMARY OF KEY POINTS

> The rules of grammar and punctuation support and give emphasis to language and help to convey its meaning.

> Spelling strategies such as using mnemonics help to develop spelling skills.

> We need to provide learners with a model of good practice in grammar, punctuation and spelling.

> Appropriate error analysis marking will encourage learners to take responsibility for their own language and literacy development.

Branching options

The following tasks are designed to help you consolidate and develop the learning points covered in this chapter.

Reflection

Consider the most effective ways in which you can encourage your learners to be self-critical of their spelling and punctuation. Note some strategies in your journal, and try them out with one of your groups.

Analysis

Review the handouts and written materials that you have designed for your learners. Check that they are grammatically correct with accurate punctuation and spelling.

Research

One difficulty associated with grammar is understanding the meaning of many of the words used to describe it. Research the concepts of *morphology, lexicology*, *semantics* and *syntax* in the context of English grammar. In what ways can an understanding of these concepts help in giving literacy support to learners?

REFERENCES AND FURTHER READING REFERENCES AND FURTHER READING

Bryson, B (2007) *Shakespeare*. London: HarperCollins.

Crystal, D (2004) *The stories of English*. London: Allen Lane.

Davidson, G (2005) *How to punctuate*. London: Penguin.

Gowers, E (1954) *The complete plain words.* London: Penguin.

Hilton, C and Hyde, M (1992) *Getting to grips with spelling*. London: Letts.

Palmer, R (1993) *Write in style*: *a guide to good English*. London: Chapman and Hall.

Truss, L (2003) *Eats, shoots and leaves*: *the zero tolerance approach to punctuation*. London: Profile Books.

Wakelin, M (1988) *The archaeology of English*. London: BT Batsford.

12
Next steps

This chapter will help you to:

- consider ways to develop your own literacy and language skills in the future, perhaps as part of your continuing professional development (CPD).

Links to LLUK Professional Standards for QTLS:
AK4.2, AK4.3, AP4.2, AP4.3, AK5.1, AP5.1, AS4, AS7, BS2, BS3, BK2.2, BK2.3, BP2.2, BP2.3, BK5.1, BK5.2, BP5.1, BP5.2, CK3.3, CK3.4, CP3.3, CP3.4, EK4.1, EP4.1, FK1.1, FK1.2, FP1.1, FP1.2, FK2.1, FP2.1, FK4.1, FK4.2, FP4.1, FP4.2.

Links to LLUK mandatory units of assessment:
Planning and enabling learning (CTLLS and DTLLS):
- understand and demonstrate knowledge of the minimum core in own practice;
- understand how reflection, evaluation and feedback can be used to develop own good practice.

Theories and principles for planning and enabling learning (DTLLS):
- understand and demonstrate knowledge of the minimum core in own practice;
- understand and demonstrate how to evaluate and improve own practice, with reference to theories and principles of learning and communication.

Introduction

So what next? If you have been with me all the way through this book, you know and understand the language and literacy minimum core and have reviewed your personal skills of reading, writing, listening and speaking. But this is only the beginning, and in some respects your journey is just starting. The challenge is to use and develop your knowledge, understanding and skills to help your learners develop their full potential and achieve their aspirations in whatever area they choose. Language and literacy must not be a barrier, but a vehicle that will enable them to work, study and communicate effectively.

This final chapter gives some pointers towards how you can use your knowledge and understanding of literacy in your professional practice once you have achieved QTLS. Some of the themes that have been introduced in the previous chapters are developed in more detail as guidance for your future. These themes are:

- maintaining an inclusive learning environment;
- identifying language and literacy needs;
- embedding language and literacy into your specialist area in a meaningful way;
- resources available to meet these needs.

In short, this is about your professional future, and is intended to help you on your way as you progress through your teaching career. Let's set the scene with a hypothetical situation.

SCENARIO STUDY – IMAGINE...

It is 11.00 a.m. on a miserable November morning. You are in your first term of teaching in an FE college, and enjoying your coffee break when you get a message from your line manager. A colleague who teaches other groups in your subject area has been involved in a car accident and will be off work for several weeks. The message asks you to teach, and generally look after, one of the level 3 groups that is now without a teacher. As this will generate some extra income, you welcome the prospect, and in return receive a folder containing the scheme of work, background on the learners and some notes from your colleague.

The scheme of work looks fine. You have no worries about the specialist content you will deliver, as you have been taking a parallel class as part of your own timetable. The notes, however, give you pause for thought. Here they are.

> *This isn't a bad group, 15 students who are mostly keen to learn. Juan and Carmen, both from Mexico, are very bright, but their English is a bit flaky, and I'm not sure that they understand everything I say. Also Darren is dyslexic and I reckon will need some support. Tracey, Gill and Paul are getting anxious about giving a presentation as part of Assignment 2, and I promised to talk to them before the end of this week. Assignment 1 has just been handed in, and should be in the submissions folder.*

Off you go to have a look at the assignments, and when you start to mark them it occurs to you that there are a few issues to sort out. Of the 15 scripts, three have a lot of spelling mistakes, two more are very badly organised, with no clear structure or paragraphing, and most of the learners have no idea of how to use apostrophes. Juan and Carmen have submitted almost identical scripts, and moreover, have clearly not understood the question!

It's pretty clear to you that most of these learners are experiencing language and literacy problems which will have a detrimental effect on their progress unless something is done about it. Fortunately, this is just week six of a 30-week programme, so at least there is time to tackle the problem.

When you think about it, there is much more to this situation than correcting spelling mistakes and giving advice on how to write assignments. It raises the whole question of how teachers can maintain an inclusive approach, can identify and integrate language and literacy needs in a meaningful way into teaching a specialist subject, and use the available support to help them do it.

Maintaining an inclusive learning environment

The companion guide summarises the theme of inclusivity very clearly.

The delivery of learning should engage, motivate and enthuse individual learners and encourage their active participation, leading to learner autonomy. This means taking individual learner needs into account and the use of a wide range of strategies, including those that take account of learners' levels of literacy [and] language.

(LLUK, November 2007, p26)

One of the themes of this book has been to focus on the individual language and literacy needs of each learner, needs that arise out of their different levels of skill, their personal barriers, their motivation, their cultural expectations, their previous experience and knowledge. We also need to bear in mind that learners will have varying levels of development within their language and literacy skills (spiky profiles). A key starting point for maintaining an inclusive environment that will take individual learner needs into account is planning and delivering differentiated learning activities. In the scenario above, Juan, Carmen, Darren, Tracey, Gill and Paul – indeed all the learners in the class – have individual literacy strengths and weaknesses that need to be considered.

The companion guide suggests that we can differentiate in a number of ways: through learning outcomes, tasks/activities, teaching/learning methods and learner groupings. In section six (pp26–36) a number of suggestions for teaching strategies are given, including:

- using learning resources at more than one level of difficulty;
- mixed ability group work;
- group work at different levels;
- extension activities for stronger learners;
- personal research;
- additional support for individuals or small groups.

This section of the guide gives more detail of these strategies with examples of good practice and links to other sources of support. It is a particularly useful resource if you are faced with a situation similar to that described in the scenario.

Identifying language and literacy needs

In the scenario, you are asked to react to a situation where problems are already evident and, in effect, adopt a reactive approach to help your learners succeed in their course. This often happens in real life – it has certainly happened to me – and we often don't have the luxury of being able to plan in a holistic way and to have access to all the support we would like.

Nevertheless, there are models of good practice that we can use as guides to give support to learners. One of the most useful is *The Learning Journey*, written for the DfES as part of the national Skills for Life programme (www.dcsf.gov.uk/readwriteplus), which emphasises that learners do not just require help with language and literacy in the classes that they attend, but that this should be part of a support system that encompasses their total learning experience. It identifies the following stages where opportunities exist for language and literacy development.

Initial assessment

Initial assessment is used to identify learners' language levels and ensure that they are enrolled on an appropriate course. In the scenario, the initial assessment should ensure that the learners' language skills are such that they can cope with a level 3 course of study.

Diagnostic assessment

Diagnostic assessment gives a detailed personal profile, indicating specific language and literacy strengths and weaknesses and highlighting any skills gaps. It provides the basis for an individual learning plan.

Individual Learning Plan (ILP)

This is a plan that is negotiated with the learner and is an outcome of the initial and diagnostic assessment process. It identifies the areas that need to be developed by the individual learner and includes an action plan for achieving the desired outcomes. The ILP is developed and monitored throughout the programme of study.

Assessment

This includes both formative assessment (to review progress) and summative assessment (to give feedback on achievement).

So, in the scenario, you have come into the middle of this process – the journey is already under way. To give the most effective support, you would need access to the results of the initial assessments, the diagnostic assessments and the ILPs of the learners you are about to meet. This would enable you to identify and assess their language and literacy needs and to plan your teaching accordingly.

It is likely that the initial and diagnostic assessments will have been carried out by a literacy specialist, and therefore your main interest is in interpreting the results. However, if you would like to research this aspect further, there is plenty of material available. The Quality Improvement Agency (QIA) publishes a range of booklets through the Skills for Life Improvement Programme (SfLIP), and booklet no. 3, entitled *Initial and diagnostic assessment* (2008), is a very useful guide which can be downloaded from www.sflip.org.uk. Another useful source of material on initial assessment is the Tools Library website, www.toolslibrary.co.uk. Their booklet *Good practice guidelines in skills check and initial assessment* is downloadable from the site, and hard-copy examples of their generic literacy assessment tools are available free of charge from the Department for Innovation, Universities and Skills (DIUS) publications at 0845 6022260.

Embedding language and literacy into your specialist area in a meaningful way

The situation in the scenario poses an important problem for you as a specialist subject teacher. Your learners have no difficulty understanding the specialist content of the programme, but are hindered by limitations in their language and literacy skills. You know that any attempt to arrange or give discrete literacy support is likely to be a de-motivating strategy which will probably be met with comments such as, *What do we have to do this for? We came to learn site management, not how to construct sentences!* The secret is to integrate literacy support into the specialist content so that your learners understand that the literacy aspects are an essential stepping-stone to their success in their chosen field.

So how do you do this? Let us assume that the first part of the process, the identification of literacy needs through initial and diagnostic assessment, has been done. The next step is a planning process, which is determined by this need and the literacy demands and level of your subject. I hope that this book has helped you in solving specific problems, such as those posed by Juan and his friends in the scenario. But it is equally important to have a strategy in place which embodies an overall and inclusive approach to literacy issues in the context of teaching a specialist subject. LLUK summarises the approach in the following way.

> *The key features of embedded practice include teamwork, staff understandings, values and beliefs, teaching and learning planning and practice as well as policies and organizational features.*

(LLUK, 2008, p4)

Such an approach encompasses good practice in any teaching situation, quite apart from the specific language and literacy issues we are considering here. But it is probably worth re-stating a few of the most important points to consider when planning your course with literacy issues in mind.

- Use a wide variety of teaching methods. This is likely to motivate learners with very different needs.
- Use communication strategies and teaching materials that are appropriate to the learners' literacy abilities and understanding.
- Design schemes of work and lesson plans with differentiated outcomes that take account of the diversity of the group and the needs of individual learners.
- Use active learning approaches in which there is a strong emphasis on learners doing things rather than being passive listeners.
- Design and use differentiated handouts and learner tasks, so that some learners can get extra support, and others can be extended with access to more advanced material.
- Ensure that language and literacy issues are taught within the specialist context.

A key starting point for any planning involving literacy support is the literacy and language requirements of your course. The course in the scenario is at level 3, so the entry level is probably level 2. So, have all these learners met this requirement, and, if so, what is the evidence? If not, what are their weaknesses and has any support been made available, either from the organisation or from your injured colleague? The course tasks in the scenario clearly include written assignments, presentations, and probably research skills. So, will this group of learners require help and support to undertake these assessments effectively? If so, could you give this help yourself, or will you need to find assistance elsewhere?

From this, it follows that you should be aware of your organisation's policy on language and literacy support. It may be, for example, that separate literacy classes are part of the provision for all learners. In any event, you need to know the specialist language and literacy support which is available and how you can access it. If you are working in a college, it is likely that a literacy specialist has already been involved with your new learners, as such a specialist will usually be responsible for the initial and diagnostic assessment. So, in this situation, you need to find out what has happened with individual learners. For example, is there any ESOL support available for Juan and Carmen, and is Darren getting specialist help with his dyslexia? Ideally, of course, this is sorted out before the course starts when problems arising from individual initial and diagnostic assessments have been identified. But even if this is not possible, at the very least you need to be aware of what help is available within your organisation.

There is an additional benefit if you are lucky enough to be working in an organisation that has effective learning support provision. You may well be able to collaborate with specialist colleagues to organise assistance in dealing with the literacy problems that you identify with this group of learners. A literacy specialist should be able to provide help to individual learners with specific literacy needs, such as Tracey, Gill and Paul, who are worried about giving presentations. You should also be able to call upon specialist literacy and language expertise to ensure that your teaching materials use language at an appropriate level for the curriculum and the abilities of your learners. At best, you will be able to work closely with literacy specialists to develop inclusive learning approaches in a collaborative way that benefits everyone – you, your learners, and your colleagues.

However, you may not be so lucky. It is very possible that you do not have specialist literacy support available, and you have to tackle these issues on your own. The good news is that there is a lot of useful material available that you can access. So, let us continue the learning journey by identifying some of this material that could help you deal with the literacy problems that you are facing in the scenario. An added benefit is that many of them are free, and can also be downloaded from the internet.

Resources for embedding language and literacy into your specialist teaching

A good starting point is the companion guide. It covers all the stages of the learning journey, and gives detailed guidance on session planning, teaching activities, resources and assessment for teachers who are embedding aspects of the minimum core into delivery of their specialist subject. It is particularly useful for the many links it gives to other resources that you may need for your own research and can be downloaded from the LLUK website or ordered free from DCSF Publications (0845 6022260).

If you need to have a detailed reference to adult literacy and ESOL, there are two documents which contain the content of all that should be taught in literacy and ESOL courses, covering three progressive levels and the skills of reading, writing, speaking and listening. These documents are the *Adult Literacy Core Curriculum* (DfES, 2001) and the *Adult ESOL Core Curriculum* (DfES, 2001). They were written as part of the national strategy to meet the literacy needs of adults, as outlined in the government discussion document *Success for All* (DfES 2002) and the White Paper *Further Education: raising Skills, Improving Life Chances* (DfES, 2006). They are intended primarily as reference documents for literacy and ESOL specialists, but provide a comprehensive and detailed source of information about language and literacy within the framework of the national standards for adult literacy. In the scenario they would be a really useful resource in designing material to help Darren and the other learners with language problems, and in embedding language and literacy elements into your specialist subject area. The core curricula are available free of charge from DCSF Publications (0845 6022260), or downloadable from the DCSF website at www.dcsf.gov.uk/publications.

There are also a number of documents that cover embedding literacy and language into vocational courses. One of the most useful sources is the DfES Embedded Learning Materials project that has now developed materials for over a dozen vocational settings. These can be accessed via the DfES embedded learning portal at http://rwp.qia.oxi.net/embeddedlearning. There is also a National Research and Development Council report, *Embedded teaching and learning of adult literacy, numeracy and ESOL* (NRDC, 2005), which contains case studies from a variety of curriculum areas, including Horticulture, Construction, Childcare, Nursing and Sports Studies. This is downloadable from www.nrdc.org.uk. A wide range of Skills for Life embedded learning materials, issued by the Quality Improvement Agency's (QIA) Skills for Life Improvement Programme, can be obtained through the programme website at www.sflip.org.uk. All in all, you should be able to find something relevant to your area of specialisation by a search of these websites.

Finally, in the context of your CPD, you may be interested in further study around the concept of embedding language and literacy into your specialist area. LLUK has developed programme specifications in this area. Units relating to an embedded approach to literacy, language and numeracy are available as optional units within DTLLS. You can access details via the LLUK website.

A SUMMARY OF KEY POINTS

> Language and literacy issues need to be considered throughout the whole of the learning journey.

> Find out about your learners' literacy/language skills through initial and diagnostic assessment.

> Negotiate a learning plan with individual learners (ILP) on the basis of these assessment results.

> Plan your teaching to take account of the language and literacy abilities of your learners.

> Find out what specialist literacy support is available.

> Integrate language and literacy within your specialist teaching.

> Collaborate with literacy specialists, wherever possible, in the planning and delivery of your programme.

> Research, and use, materials that are appropriate for embedding literacy in your subject area.

Postscript

I have always been conscious that teaching can be fraught and stressful, but also immensely rewarding. This final chapter brings me to the end of a stage in my own learning journey, and I've discovered that writing a book generates much the same emotions.

I also know that good teachers change learners' lives, invariably for the better. My hope is that this book has helped you on your learning journey and given you a greater understanding of language and literacy. I hope too, that it will help you to support your learners on their journey through the complex world of lifelong learning.

REFERENCES AND FURTHER READING REFERENCES AND FURTHER READING

DfES (2001) *Adult ESOL Core Curriculum.* London: DfES.

DfES (2001) *Adult Literacy Core Curriculum.* London: DfES.

DfES (2006) *Further Education: Raising Skills, Improving Life Chances.* London: DfES.

DfES (2006) *Good Practice Guidelines in Skills Check and Initial Assessment.* London: DfES.

DfES (2002) *Success for All.* London: DfES.

LLUK (November 2007) *Inclusive learning approaches for literacy, language, numeracy and ICT.* London: LLUK (the companion guide).

LLUK (2008) *Level 5 award in developing embedded approaches to literacy, language and numeracy for teachers in the lifelong learning sector.* London: LLUK.

NRDC (2005) *Embedded teaching and learning of adult literacy, numeracy and ESOL.* London: NRDC.

QIA (2008) *Guidance for assessment and learning – initial and diagnostic assessment; a learner-centred approach.* London: QIA.

Websites

www.dcsf.gov.uk/readwriteplus/teachingandlearning
www.dius.gov.uk
www.goldust.org.uk
www.lluk.org.uk
www.nrdc.org.uk
www.qia.org.uk
www.sflip.org.uk
www.toolslibrary.co.uk

Appendix 1
Summary of the minimum core for language and literacy elements

A 1   Personal, social and cultural factors influencing language and literacy learning and development:

A 1.1   The different factors affecting the acquisition and development of language and literacy skills.

A 1.2   The importance of English language and literacy in enabling users to participate in public life, society and the modern economy.

A 1.3   Potential barriers that can hinder development of language skills.

A 1.4   The main learning disabilities and difficulties relating to language learning and skill development.

A 1.5   Multilingualism and the role of the first language in the acquisition of additional languages.

A 1.6   Issues that arise when learning another language or translating from one language to another.

A 1.7   Issues related to varieties of English, including standard English, dialects and attitudes towards them.

A 1.8   The importance of context in language use and the influence of the communicative situation.

A 2   Explicit knowledge about language and of the four skills: speaking, listening, reading and writing:

Speaking:

A 2.1   Making appropriate choices in oral communication episodes.

A 2.2   Having a knowledge of fluency, accuracy and competence for ESOL learners.

A 2.3   Using spoken English effectively.

Listening:

A 2.4   Listening effectively.

Reading:

A 2.5   Interpreting written texts.

A 2.6   Knowledge of how textual features support reading.

A 2.7   Understanding the barriers to accessing text.

Writing:

A 2.8   Communicating the writing process.

A 2.9   Using genre to develop writing.

A 2.10 Developing spelling and punctuation skills.

B   Personal language skills:

Speaking:

B 1   Expressing yourself clearly, using communication techniques to help convey meaning and to enhance the delivery and accessibility of the message.

B 2   Showing the ability to use language, style and tone in ways that suit the intended audience, and to recognise their use by others.

B 3   Using appropriate techniques to reinforce oral communication, check how well the information is received and support the understanding of those listening.

B 4   Using non-verbal communication to assist in conveying meaning and receiving information, and recognising its use by others.

Listening:

B 5   Listening attentively and responding sensitively to contributions made by others.

Reading:

B 6   Find, and select from, a range of reference material and sources of information, including the internet.

B 7   Use and reflect on a range of reading strategies to interpret texts and to locate information or meaning.

B 8   Identify and record the key information or messages contained within reading material using note-making techniques.

Writing:

B 9   Write fluently, accurately and legibly on a range of topics.

B 10   Select appropriate format and style of writing for different purposes and different readers.

B 11   Use spelling and punctuation accurately in order to make meaning clear.

B 12   Understand and use the conventions of grammar (the forms and structures of words, phrases, clauses, sentences and texts) consistently when producing written text.

Appendix 2
Checklist of minimum core elements against chapter contents

Chapter	1	2	3	4	5	6	7	8	9	10	11	12
Element Knowledge and Understanding:												
A1.1		X	X	X	X							
A1.2		X		X	X				X			
A1.3		X	X	X	X							
A1.4		X		X	X							
A1.5		X				X						
A1.6		X				X						
A1.7		X				X						
A1.8		X	X									
A2.1		X					X					
A2.2		X					X					
A2.3		X					X					
A2.4		X					X	X				
A2.5		X							X			
A2.6		X							X			
A2.7		X							X			
A2.8		X								X	X	
A2.9		X								X		
A2.10		X									X	
Personal skills: Speaking												
B1		X					X	X				
B2		X					X					
B3		X					X	X				
B4		X						X				
Listening												
B5	X						X	X				
Reading												
B6	X								X			
B7	X								X			
B8	X								X			
Writing												
B9	X									X	X	
B10	X									X		
B11	X									X	X	
B12	X									X	X	

Appendix 3
Glossary of acronyms

ATLS Associate Teacher, Learning and Skills; the professional status awarded to those LS teachers who are working in an associate teaching role.

CAT Credit Accumulation and Transfer; a system that allows learners to save and transfer credit achieved within the Qualifications and Credit Framework.

CPD Continuing Professional Development; activity undertaken to develop professional knowledge or teaching skills.

CTLLS Certificate in Teaching in the Lifelong Learning Sector; the qualification for teachers in the associate teaching role.

DCSF Department for Children, Schools and Families.

DDA Disability Discrimination Act; the 1995 Act banned most providers of goods, services and facilities from treating disabled people less favourably because of their disability, and the 2005 Act gave public authorities a duty to promote disability equality.

DfES Department for Education and Skills; replaced in 2007 by the Department for Innovation, Universities and Skills and the Department for Children, Schools and Families.

DIUS Department for Innovation, Universities and Skills.

DTLLS Diploma in Teaching in the Lifelong Learning Sector; the qualification for teachers in the full teaching role.

ESOL English for Speakers of Other Languages.

IfL Institute for Learning; the professional body responsible for conferring licensed practitioner status for teachers in the lifelong learning sector.

LLUK Lifelong Learning UK; the Sector Skills Council for lifelong learning.

NRDC National Research and Development Centre; a consortium led by the Institute for Learning conducting research and development into adult literacy and other aspects of the minimum core.

PTLLS Preparing to Teach in the Lifelong Learning Sector; the first unit of both CTLLS and DTLLS, conferring a threshold licence to practise.

QCA Qualifications and Curriculum Authority; the organisation that oversees the National Qualifications Framework.

QIA Quality Improvement Agency; the agency responsible for providing funds and programmes to raise the quality of education within the lifelong learning sector.

QTLS Qualified Teacher Learning and Skills; the professional status awarded to those LS teachers who are working in a full teaching role.

SENDA The Special Educational Needs and Disability Act 2001; extended the 1995 Disability Discrimination Act to education providers, making it illegal for them to treat disabled learners less favourably because of their disability.

SfL Skills for Life; the strategy to support adult literacy, numeracy and ESOL, initiated in 2001 in response to the Moser Report.

SfLIP Skills for Life Improvement Programme; programmes and resources to support the Skills for Life strategy.

SVUK Standards Verification UK; subsidiary of LLUK, responsible for the endorsement and verification of ITT programmes within the lifelong learning sector.

Index

Added to a page number 'f' denotes a figure.